•THE 7th LIST
•OF SHIT
•THAT MADE
•ME A
•FEMINIST

Farida D.

Farida D. is an Arab gender researcher and poet, studying Arab women's everyday oppressions for over a decade. Through the process- she broke up with her hijab, set her high heels on fire, and authored a series of books. Farida's words have been on BBC Radio London, are continuously amplified by celebrities, and strolling all over social media. Contact her via email farida-d@outlook.com, or on Instagram @farida.d.author

This is for the women
who have been doubted.

I see you.
I hear you.
I believe you.
I am you.

And there's an army of us.

1201.

The
deepest
darkest
loneliest
thoughts
that run through your blood
are from the wounds of a sisterhood
that has been silenced, for centuries,
by the patriarchy
with the goal of making you,
doubt your sanity.

I feel you, when you feel
alone.
Together, sister,
we can walk back home.

1202.

"Women have their rights
to vote, to study, to work.
What more do you want?"
he asks.

"I want all of it",
I tell him with insatiable greed.
"I want everything you have
everything you want
everything you need-
I want my egg
to be as worthy as your seed,
I want to keep on fighting
until every woman is freed".

***

We got this.

Gone are the days women eat
platefuls of silence.
We will roar
and we will rip
off the bandages
covering up for
men's violence.

We got this.

1203.

There is no woman in the world
who is not a feminist.
She may not like the label
but, from its labour, she benefits.

Can you read this?
Feminists fought for your right to read.

Can you make your own life choices?
Feminists fought to give you voices.

Can you do whatever you want with your body?
Feminists fought to reclaim that too.

You can say you're not a feminist,
but you can never deny that you benefit
from the labour of the women who fought for you.

***

The people offended
by feminism,
are the reason
we need feminism.

1204.

You know what's scarier
than the men who are actually
wolves dressed as men?
The women who are actually
wolves dressed as women.

Because while you might expect this from men
who are dressed up by the patriarchy,
you don't see it coming from women.

A woman who devours
her oppression like a feast-
is fucking scarier
than the oppressive beast,
because she is willing to do
everything she's told;
to go against her own gender
to insidiously uphold
her own oppressor,
just to hold
a little bit of (pseudo) power.

She'd do anything to pay the rent
for that Ivory Tower.

What she doesn't know is that
no matter how much she's willing to pay;
that Ivory Tower is a temporary stay.
It will never be hers to own
it belongs to the men, built by them
and only for them,

and just like the men decide
if she can stay
the men will decide
to kick her out any day.
Because when the rent increases
(and it always does)
and she struggles to pay
she will painfully see-
that a woman can never
(without losing herself)
win over,
the patriarchy.

***

Women are rewarded by men
for being complicit in their own misogyny.

And so when you are reaping a reward
it becomes really hard
to pay attention to how it's hurting you too.

It's like staying in a job
where you are mistreated,
but you still stay for the money it pays you.

1205.

To the woman who voted for patriarchy,
do you understand that you will never
attain any victory?
So why do you do it
when it hurts you and me?
It is to be loved by the men?
To be accepted and praised by them?
Or are you simply unaware
of your internalized misogyny?
Do you know you are worth so much more
than the lies that men
use to lock your door?
Is that all you ever want?
To be pawn in a game
that will always taunt
you, your mother, your sister, your aunt?

Can't you see?

There is NO
special place
in the patriarchy
for women
who vote
against
other women.

N.B. But "there is a special place in hell for women who don't help
other women"- Madeleine Albright.

1206.

All women benefit from feminism,
for it has given us all a voice-
even the women who loudly proclaim
they aren't feminists.

All men benefit from patriarchy,
for it gives them all a voice-
even the men who loudly proclaim
they aren't bad guys.

1207.

They want you to believe
that saying ALL MEN
is a generalization,
yet isn't saying NOT ALL MEN
also a generalization?

1208.

 "NOT ALL MEN!"
he would scream;
"don't generalize
one man's behaviour
does not represent all of us!"

"FEMINISM IS NO LONGER NEEDED!"
he would also scream;
"I never hurt women,
and I don't know any man who does!"

So for men's predatory behaviour,
we *shouldn't* generalize
but for men's non-predatory behaviour,
we *should* generalize?
You cannot cherry-pick
out of strawberry pies;
if generalization is wrong
then it is wrong all along.

Not all men are dressed in lies
but feminism is still needed
to combat those in disguise.

1209.

You say;
it's not all men.
I ask you;
which one of them then?
Point them out for me.
Isolate them, ostracize them
guarantee my safety.

You say;
it's not all men.
I tell you;
I don't know
which man out of all men
will assault me
will beat me
will rape me
will murder me.
I am wary
of all men
to keep myself in safety
from that hidden one
or some
of them.

You say;
but it offends and hurts me
because I'm a good guy.
I say;
but are you really a good guy,
if the male ego

is more important to you
than if a woman would die?

You say;
how can I prove to you then?
I say;
you don't have to prove it to me
instead prove it to other men,
the ones who do harm to my gender
in the name of upholding your power
prove to them
that there are ways to be men
without being toxic
without ruining it for all men.

1210.

To the men who *speak out* for women
because they have mothers, sisters, daughters, and wives;
can you, instead, *speak to* the men?
Because you have fathers, brothers,
sons, and friends,
that are ruining our lives.

The problem isn't that men
say NOT ALL MEN,
it's that they say it *to women*
instead of to other men.

1211.

When a human
walks next to a free flock of birds
the birds will almost always flee,
this natural response is based on
trauma from experience and ancestry.
The free bird does not know
which human is merely
passing, and which
is preying on its captivity.

Remember that next time you're inclined
to say NOT ALL MEN;
because women don't know
which one it could be.

1212.

While I cannot walk home safely
some dude on the internet
thinks my lack of safety is equivalent
to his ego being crushed
because I didn't say "not all men"...

***

It should not be
a privilege
to walk home safely.

Tonight
we light candles for a vigil,
but tomorrow
we'll burn down the entire city.

N.B. Sarah Everard.

1213.

When a woman hears
about another woman
abused by a man
she thinks; *it could have been me.*

When a man hears
about a woman
abused by another man
he screams; *NOT ME- NOT ALL MEN!*

And that's the problem
core and centre;
while women sympathize
men refuse to even recognize,
the hurt caused by their own gender.

N.B. This hurt caused by your gender is because of entitlement. And
you refusing to recognize it is because of entitlement.

1214.

Not all men will attack women,
but all men are *safe* to do so.
Because the patriarchy
protects all men,
and they all
fucking know.

All men have a privilege in the patriarchy
that comes with their gender
as a birthright;
whether they use it or not
whether they see it or not,
it's like living in darkness
but having a flashlight.

Saying "ALL MEN" is not an insult,
it is an acknowledgement of reality.

Saying "ALL MEN" doesn't mean "all men are bad";
it means ALL MEN ARE PROTECTED BY PATRIARCHY.

N.B. Out of every 1000 sexual assaults, 955 perpetrators will walk
free. (Source: The Criminal Justice System statistics by RAINN-
Rape, Abuse & Incest National Network).

1215.

How dare you tell me
NOT ALL MEN,
when I know
that even
the men I love
my husband, my father
my son, my brother
can (if they want to) fuck me up,
and they know (and I know)
there is an entire system
built by the men before them
to back ALL MEN up!

ALL MEN
benefit from patriarchy.

1216.

Why it is ALL MEN:

*ALL MEN are given privileges by patriarchy (whether they use them or not) that are assigned to their gender at the expense of non-men.

*ALL MEN are conditioned to normalize both misogyny and toxic masculinity. Even the men brought up in non-misogynistic and non-toxic households are still exposed to that shit elsewhere (in schools, workplaces, books, media, laws, etc.).

*ALL MEN are protected by patriarchy should they impart misogyny.

*ALL MEN are hurt by patriarchy should they practice toxic masculinity (hurt on themselves and/or other men).

*ALL MEN also benefit from the prevalence of toxic masculinity because it means that any man can just do the bare minimum (e.g. not assault women) to be considered a "nice guy".

*ALL MEN can use the privileges given to them by patriarchy to actively fight against misogyny and toxic masculinity.

1217.

Building your entire argument on the origins of patriarchy down to "men being physically stronger" is completely flawed and misinformed. Look into the Neolithic revolution which is where patriarchy started. Before that we were hunter/gatherers and life was egalitarian. When we moved to farming, birth rates increased due to being settled (more time for sex) and as women were constantly going through pregnancy/childbirth, men managed the farming property. And that's when men started to "control" the financial resources and pass it down the male line, leaving nothing to women and treating them as merely another resource to control (to bring more children to be used as labour in the farm). And that is why we still have stigmas on abortion (patriarchy wants to keep pushing women into motherhood roles and out of public spaces). And that's also the birth of modesty/virginity/purity culture where a woman's sexuality is controlled to ensure a man passes his property to an heir that is his own blood. It is also from this patriarchal system that capitalism and racism emerged; men who owned property had power over men who didn't, and Black people were enslaved to be used as free labour. I could go on. The harms of the patriarchy invade our ideologies and lifestyles to this day. And so, NO it is not because "men are physically stronger". But that's a nice story to tell your ego.

1218.

It is a sustainable strategy
for men to blame patriarchy
on nature,
or a deity.

Because logically,
how can we
question biology,
or get answers
from a non-responsive
divine?

But I believe
that nature and God
are both victims of patriarchy too,
and men have been victim blaming
since the dawn of time.

1219.

Saying that patriarchy exists
because men are naturally superior over women
is as ridiculous as
saying that racism exists
because Whites are naturally superior over Blacks.

We are all born
out of the *same*
union of equality
between a sperm and an egg.

There is nothing natural to us about inequality.

1220.

When I say the patriarchy hurts women,
it doesn't mean that the patriarchy
doesn't hurt men.

When I say the patriarchy is upheld by men
it doesn't mean that the patriarchy
isn't upheld by women.

In discussions, we should focus
on each problem separately
and give each point its own devotion.
Because each problem
has a different solution.

1221.

All men benefit from patriarchy
this is irrefutably true;
and that's exactly why
they can't see
how patriarchy hurts them too.

All men benefit from patriarchy.
But all men are also hurt by patriarchy.
Because to benefit men need to first pay-
patriarchal benefits aren't offered for free.
Men pay by buying notions of unrealistic masculinity;
their payment includes stripping from their emotions,
they become violent and toxic
thus technically to be misogynistic,
men must first embrace misandry
without a fight.

Feminism is for everybody
because the patriarchy
treats none of us right.

1222.

How dismantling the patriarchy benefits males and men:

Patriarchy privileges males and men by treating them as above everyone else simply because of their sex and gender.

BUT upholding patriarchy and gaining privilege is not free. Males and men must pay a price to keep the system well and alive, and to be seen as and treated as "real men" by the patriarchy. This price comes in the form of following a certain narrative;
-men must be tough, show no emotions besides anger
-men must carry the burden of being the main breadwinners
-men must uphold a heteronormative narrative
etc.

What does paying this price cost for males and men? Here are a few examples:
-Increased illness rates because of refusing to seek medical help when needed to avoid being seen as weak.
-Increased suicide rates because of refusing to seek therapy and repressing emotions.
-Increased death rates because of drinking and traffic accidents to uphold the immortal tough macho man narrative.

The issues men face are the cost of upholding their privilege. Which is why dismantling the patriarchy serves everyone!

N.B. Recommended reading: Pan American Health Organization. *Masculinities and Health in the Region of the Americas. Executive Summary.* Washington, D.C.: PAHO; 2019.

1223.

It is important to note that whatever struggle males and men face in the patriarchy does not override the privilege they are afforded which non-males and non-men do not have. The struggles that face males and men are because they have to perform a certain narrative to get rewarded with the privilege. This can backfire. For example, because men are expected to be the strong/powerful gender, it is believed they are the rapist not the raped (and if the situation is otherwise, men's trauma is dismissed). That is how systems of privilege hurt everyone, and why they should be dismantled by everyone.

1224.

I tell him "you're unlike all men".
And he tells me "you're not like other girls".

And it's easier for us pretend
that those are compliments,
instead of confront
our gendered trauma and torment.

***

"Not all men!"
"Not like other girls!"

In both, an individual is seeking to
separate from the narcissistic
stigma of their group
in order to not be blamed.
Yet ironically, in doing so,
a "pick-me" egotistical behaviour
is perpetuated
and that narcissistic stigma is sustained.

N.B. Compliments rooted in sexism are not compliments; they are
still sexism.

1225.

Patriarchy teaches men
that there is only one way
to be a real man,
while it teaches women
to only desire
that "real man".

Patriarchy teaches women
to be in service for men
offer free care for them,
while it teaches men
to view it as the duty of a woman
to provide service and free care to man.

***

In any situations
where men experience suppressions
women experience it worse.

Thus when we liberate women
we liberate everyone
from the patriarchal curse.

1226.

The patriarchy privileges men
by viewing them
as superior, stronger, breadwinners,
but as a result it hurts them
by expecting them
to never be emotional, vulnerable, or soft.

The patriarchy oppresses women
by viewing them
as inferior, weaker, homemakers,
and as a result it hurts them
by expecting them
to never be superior, stronger, breadwinners,
independent, rational, or hard.

That is why, by the patriarchy,
both men and women are scarred.

That is why
men are expected to fight wars,
but women will more likely win battles
of child custody.

That is why
men are expected to work
the outdoor dangerous jobs,
but women are more likely
to never be free.

1227.

I think feminism
and men's rights activism
aren't separate categories.

They fight one another
but fail to see,
that they have one enemy:

Patriarchy.

1228.

Can men be feminists? Or can they only ever be allies?

They can be both.

Can men ever directly experience the patriarchal trauma that results from femicide, honour killings, lack of anatomical science focused on their bodies, female genital mutilation, period and maternity discrimination, slut shaming and purity culture, dress codes, and the endless list of shit that ONLY women experience?

No.

So in those spaces men can only ever be allies. By that I mean they can listen, hold space, work on solutions that women need- but they can't talk over us or tell us how to solve these issues.

However, can men directly experience the patriarchal trauma that results from toxic masculinity, societal expectations of manhood, circumcision normalization, and the endless list of shit that exists because "to be a man" must be so remotely distinct from the slightest thing that is related to "being a woman"?

Yes.

So in those spaces men can be feminists. Because by fighting misogyny they liberate themselves too. How so?!

The endless list of shit for men "to be a man" exists *because of misogyny*, because patriarchy hates women and so men must not resemble women. Men aren't expected to show emotions, vulnerability, participate in childcare, wear dresses or pink or makeup or be interested in fashion, or receive penetration- because those things are associated with women. Those expectations are also the seeds of toxic masculinity. Toxic masculinity is more about *how not to be a woman* than *how to be a man*.

Thus by being a feminist in those spaces (through dismantling misogyny) men can create world where no man will be stigmatized for doing what is deemed as "for women" (because whatever is "for women" will no longer be stigmatized either when we dismantle misogyny), and thus no man will be expected to behave in a certain way to be considered a "real man". In this way the notion of toxic masculinity is eradicated.

1229.

When we say
MEN CAN'T BE FEMINISTS
what we actually mean
is that men will never know
the pain women go through
(not that we don't know
that the patriarchy
hurts men too).

The patriarchy hurts men
but it just hurts them
because that's the price
they must pay to get to the benefits.
Whereas when
the patriarchy hurts women
it does it purely so that
only the patriarchy profits.

Men can't be feminists-
because men can reap benefits
from their suppression,
and if they don't want suppression
they have the power to end their patriarchal subscription.
Whereas women can only get
oppression,
and are forced to hold
membership
unless they fight to be feminists.

Men can't be feminists,
but here's the twist-

it doesn't mean
that men can't be
liberated by
feminism.

1230.

If you are non-Black,
you will never know
what it's like
living in Black skin,
so you can only ever be
a Black ally.

If you are non-disabled,
you will never know
what's like
living with a disability,
so you can only ever be
a disability ally.

If you are non-queer
you will never know
what's like
living as a queer,
so you can only ever be
an LGBTQI+ ally.

And if you are a non-woman,
you will never know
what it's like
living as a woman,
so you can only ever be
a feminist ally.

1231.

Feminism isn't obligated
to give space for men
who want to be feminists-
because feminism is about
reclaiming the space
that men stole from us.

But men who want
to be feminists
are obligated
to give space for feminism-
and to do that
they *must*
give back the space
they stole from us.

Men have been *hoarding* space
paid for by women's oppression.
For change,
men must be *holding* space for our feminism.

1232.

What if
men don't even apply
to candidacy
for presidency...?

What if,
for one term,
they decide to leave
the entire space
for women?

Instead of applying alongside us
and winning over us
because they always will win
if the choice is between
a man or a woman...

What if men
don't apply at all?

What if they take a stance
to stand back
and watch women stand tall?

Imagine.

Imagine not having
to fight men over a seat,
because they are willing to sit back
without seeing it as a defeat.

Women have been sitting back
(and have been pushed back)
by men and for men
to rule the world.
Why can't men, for one term,
let our voices be heard?

The patriarchy
won't ever be
dismantled,
if men don't stand back
to give us back
some of the space
they have been hoarding.

It's like a flight
where at the gate,
only men are always boarding.

How can a woman fly
if a man won't give up his seat
to give her a turn to now see the world?

They want us to fight for a seat
while they calmly stand there
knowing they will win it.

Because while
women are fighting for the seat,
only men are allowed
to actually buy a ticket.

Think about it.

1233.

It's almost always other women
who actively perform unpaid labour of educating men
on feminism.

Where are the good men?
Where are our allies?
I know you're there!

Can you speak up??
Talk to your buddies; don't just tell me you care!

Being an ally requires action
and we need you to speak out
with our same passion!

1234.

Teach your sons
that the dragons and monsters
that the prince has to fight
to get to the princess
in fairytales-
are actually
symbolic of the real life
toxic masculinity and misogyny
that the patriarchy entails.

Teach your sons
that this is how they win
the heart of a woman-
that until they speak out against misogyny
in every form, it prevails.

So that if your boys become men
they will know then
that each time they say nothing
to their friends
who are toxic misogynistic shits,
they let the monsters of misogyny
grow stronger by being complicit.

1235.

Men's violence against women
is often shortened to
"violence against women"
and not only does this reduction
remove the perpetrator,
but the absence of men also implies that
"violence against women"
is a women's issue-
when, in fact, it is very much a men's issue.

Every injustice and discrimination
labelled as "women's issues",
is actually caused by men-
women's issues
are, at the core, men's issue!

1236.

Feminism is predominantly about
teaching women how to love themselves,
yet the movement is constantly interrupted
by men who hate women
accusing us of hating men.

At the heart of it,
all those men want from us
is to just
love them.

And to love them, precisely as they continue to hate us
so that it becomes harder for us
to love ourselves.

                              ***

And if I do hate men
why is that so bad?

For men have hated me
from the moment the doctor sighed
"it's a girl", to my dad.

1237.

What is the worst thing
a feminist can do to a man?
Hate him.

What is the worst thing
a man can do to a woman?
Kill her.

A man's oppression
is rooted in his ego.
A woman's oppression
is rooted in her survival.

N.B. "Men are afraid that women will laugh at them. Women are afraid that men will kill them." -Margaret Atwood.

1238.

Any time
I fight
for the rights
of women,
people ask whether
I hate men-
and the fact that
they even make that connection,
explains ever so succinctly
why women and their rights
have no place in the patriarchy.

If, by fighting
for women's rights
you accuse me
of hating men;
you're saying that
the only acceptable way
to love men,
is by accepting
my oppression;
which means
you're admitting
that men love
to oppress me.

***

Fighting
for women's rights
is not about hating (or loving) men;
It. Is. Not. About. Men.

If anything, it's about liberation from them.

And if wanting to be equal to men
makes men say we hate them,
then what should we say about men
who say they love us
but don't want us
to be equal to them?

1239.

Feminism is not anti-men.
It is pro-women.

And if you think pro-women is anti-men
then you are perpetuating patriarchy.
You are the problem.

There is room for all of us.

***

Feminism is pro-women
and that doesn't mean it's anti-men.

But when I am constantly interrupted to explain
that feminism is not anti-men,
it leaves no time to address the issues
of women.

To be constantly expected to talk about being pro-men
while I'm trying to talk for women,
becomes anti-women.

1240.

But I don't hate men.

I don't care whether you're born
a girl or a boy-
women deserve the same rights
that men enjoy.

But I don't hate men.

I want to fuck the patriarchy
the way it's fucking me-
I want to withhold orgasms
from toxic masculinity.

But I don't hate men.

I want to strip the internalized misogyny
off of my skin-
look in the mirror to see my beauty
and my brains within.

But I don't hate men.

Behind every great man is a great woman
they tell me-
but I want to be *beside* my man
I want equality.

But I don't hate men.

When I fight for my rights

they accuse me of hating men.
But by denying my rights,
don't they hate women?

But I don't hate men.

Each day,
they interrupt what I need to say
because all they want me to say
to them...
is;
But I don't hate men.
But I don't hate men.
But I don't hate men.
But I don't hate men.
But I don't hate men.
But I don't hate men.
But I don't hate men.
But I don't hate men.
But I don't hate men.
But I don't hate men.
But I don't hate men.
But I don't hate men.
But I don't hate men.
But I don't hate men.
But I don't hate men.
But I don't hate men.

***

If we have to keep pausing our activism
to assure men they aren't hated by feminism,
it becomes a movement not for reclaiming the rights that women are
forced to forgo-
but a movement for the massaging
of the male ego.

N.B. "I'm speaking"- Kamala Harris.

1241.

Women are insidiously
trained
to cater everything they do
to be about and for men;
from the way we dress
to the professions
we choose,
to if, and how, we raise a family;
even as we fight the patriarchy
we are asked
whether we still love men?
And how can feminism
be catered to them?

1242.

I don't hate men,
I hate their silence;
their upholding of patriarchy
their complicity
the way they claim benefits
while standing over me,
when all I'm asking for
is for them to stand by me.

If I hated men
I would fight to oppress them
I won't be fighting for equality.

***

If feminists hate men
we would be advocating for women
to make men live in fear.
The statistics by the U.N.
would say each year
that 5,000 men are killed by women in the name of honour,
and 50,000 men are killed by women in the name of horror
through intimate partner violence.
We would objectify you
until your tongues bleed silence.
The hair removal survey conducted by American Laser Centers
would say that men are expected
to spend up to $23,000 on hair removal in their lifetime.

We would expect you to spend all your fucking time
on grooming to remove your bodily hair,
and each natural bodily strength you have
would be seen as a despicable despair.

If feminists hate men
that would be our fight-
for men to live in constant fear
while doing day to day stuff,
or going for a walk at midnight.
We would constantly gaslight
victim blame, and shame,
treat your life like a monopoly game.

But you know what?
This is all stuff you do to us
and if we speak out, you make a fuss
and you accuse us of being hateful too-
we don't want revenge, all we're asking for
is to be treated with the same dignity
in which we treat you!

1243.

Men who feel threatened by feminism
are under the impression
that we want to treat men the way they treat us-
but what we want is for men
to treat us the way we treat them.

Feminism
isn't about hating men-
it's about loving women
as much as we love men.

***

If my feminism
intimidates
your masculinity;
ask yourself why
your masculinity
is contingent upon
oppressing me?

If my freedom
intimidates
your masculinity;
ask yourself why
you 'being a man'
is contingent upon
oppressing me?

And if my feminism
makes you think
I hate men;
ask yourself why
to love you,
you expect me to
hate myself?

1244.

When I was a teenager
I dumbed myself down
to make the boys love me.

It worked, like a curse, yet magically.

I noticed how they would laugh
when I was silly,
pretending to be naive
asking shit like "what's a willy?"

The smaller I made myself
the bigger they felt.
I knew how to play
the cards I was dealt.
I inflated them like balloons
that I knew how to pop-
but I also knew that if I didn't keep blowing
they would stop,
loving me.

I thought I was winning
when I made myself lose-
because then more boys wanted to be
around me
and I had more options to choose.

I really thought I was winning
it took years to see the self-abuse.

When I was a teenager

I dumbed myself down
to make the boys love me.

Such a shame that I did that
when instead
I could have
loved me.

Such a shame that I couldn't
love me.

N.B. According to research conducted by Dr Maria do Mar Pereira
from the U.K.'s University of Warwick's Department of Sociology,
girls feel they must 'play dumb' to please boys – as boys had acquired
the belief that girls should be less intelligent than them.

1245.

Men aren't *intimidated* by strong women;
they're *afraid* of them.

And so in a world that caters to man
and absolves his fears;
a woman is taught to be weak
to bow down, to bend down, to fold down
until she disappears.

***

They want to snatch away
our power
because they're scared of it.

A woman who is
unafraid to be herself,
is hated by men
because they fear
not being able
to control her.

They say "feminism is cancer"
only because
they are sickly deadly
afraid to see,
women
being
totally free.

1246.

Let him be the wolf
if he so wants
if that's what it takes
for him to feel his manhood.

But make it clear that
you are not
his *Little Red Riding hood.*

1247.

I'm the wolf.

I'm the evil villain.

At least that's how men see me
because I won't let them
oppress women.

1248.

If
I need to
shrink
to make you feel
like a big
man-
then you are not a big man.

If
to make you feel like a man,
I must, as a woman,
be less than
a human-
then fuck your manhood.

If
to feel man enough,
you need to perform your masculinity
at the expense of my oppression-
then I will never make you feel man enough
because I will never be under your submission.

And if
my feminism
turns you off;
then I never want to
turn you on.

1249.

If a vampire gets life
by sucking human blood;
who is the one
that keeps the other alive?

If a predator gets food
by eating the prey's meat;
who is the one
that keeps the other full?

If a man gets his strength
by oppressing a woman;
who is the one
that keeps the other strong?

N.B. Don't give them your power to feed on.

1250.

"I'm not a misogynist-
I don't hate women, I just hate feminists"
he says.

Can't you see?
The fact that you hate feminists
is a basic example
of your misogyny.

Because what you're saying is
"I only love women who agree with me".

N.B. Reflect on your misogyny.

1251.

And if I told you
that I hate men,
is that the worst thing
for me to say?

"Actions speak louder than words" they say.

And it is the men who say they love us
that abuse, rape, and kill us
every fucking day.

1252.

"I DON'T HATE WOMEN!"
he would cry, and then attempt to justify
"I have a mother!
A sister! A wife! A daughter!
I don't hate women!"

"But that's fucking irrelevant"
I tell him,
"especially when
study after study
would constantly
show-
that misogyny and violence
are inflicted upon women
mostly by
the *men we know*".

N.B. 137 women across the world are killed by a member of their own family every day. (Source: United Nations Office on Drugs and Crime- *Global Study on Homicide* 2018).

1253.

I'll tell you about a prison
that has imprisoned innocent women
for a very long time.
We rarely talk about it
because you don't see the problem
when you normalize the crime.

From America to China
to Dubai to Rome
they all have that prison
except they call it "home".

Do you know
how many women
in our time and day
still need permission
from a father or spouse
simply to
leave the house?
It's labelled as a form "protection"
to normalize this type of control.

Oh what a plot hole!

Do you know
how many women
in our time and day,
perform labour
inside the homes
without any monetary pay?
It's labelled as their "duty"

to normalize their exploitation.

Oh what an expectation!

There are women who get beaten,
and even killed inside their homes
by the men they love
and there are no laws to say
enough is enough,
for those are "family affairs"
and it's normalized for no one to care.

There are prisons
for women
with white dresses
and white picket fences
and fairytale dreams
turned into nightmares.

There are prisons
called "houses"-
and they are everywhere.

N.B. The home is the most likely place for a woman to be killed.
(Source: United Nations Office on Drugs and Crime- *Global Study on Homicide* 2018).

1254.

"He was just having a bad day"

That's what they say.

Oh how many times
has a woman
been told this
or convinced herself of it
to excuse or forgive
the violence of men.

That's why we struggle to say "no".
That's why we accept men's shit-show.
That's why we endure, to avoid another blow.
Because we surely fucking know
what happens when
men
are having a bad day.

N.B. Making *excuses* for the violence of men towards women, means
you are *excusing* the violence of men towards women.

1255.

We die
accidently.

Women die
accidently.

He was too angry.
He was too drunk.
She was too rebellious. '
She was too wrong.

And each headline you read
tells you all that you need
to know;
A woman has accidently died
at the hands of a man
who was angry at her
because she did so and so.

For falling in love
for having sex
for being choked
during sex
for dishonouring her family
for that mini-dress.
For whatever else.
Fill in the blanks
with whatever opposition.
Women die for doing things
without permission.

Women die
accidently,
under the hands of men
who are angry.

Women die
accidently-
but would men actually die
if they just
...let us be?

1256.

Instead of asking her;
"why did you choose to stay?"

Ask him;
"why did you choose to abuse?"

Or better yet
ask patriarchal society
how it led them to choose?

In childhood, she was taught
that the boy who hits her
secretly likes her
so she stays because she's confused.
While he was taught
that boys must never hit *girls*
(instead of never hit *anyone*)
because girls can't hit back with the same intensity.
Ironically,
he is now armed with a weapon
that he can use without repercussion
whenever he wants to attack
safe in the knowing that when he does hit a girl
she won't hit harder back.
Along with this and as a succession
he was taught that violence
is his only acceptable expression,
because feelings are only for girls
and only girls cause drama.

The reason she stayed

and the reason he abused
isn't some sci-fi panorama.

What we learn in childhood
becomes in adulthood
how we cope with trauma.

N.B. Recommended reading: *Why don't women leave abusive
relationships?* (www.womensaid.org.uk)

1257.

A man fears being rejected
by a woman he'd kill for.
A woman fears being killed
by a man she rejected.

When men ignore women,
women cry for them.
When women ignore men,
men kill them.

N.B. Look up 'Rejection killings'

1258.

Women are not
shooting ranges
for men having a bad day.
They are not
prescription medicine
for men who don't feel okay.

Women are not your punching bags
or dolls that you strip off rags.

Women are not places
for you practice your toxic masculinity,
they are not the pillars
you break
to hold up your patriarchy.

Women are not lessons
to lessen
your pain.

Don't you fucking use women
in that way again!

1259.

Women don't owe you.

Women don't owe you
their time, their unpaid labour, or space-
if you want to be an ally
take this man's world you've colonized
and make it a safe place.

Women don't owe you.

Women don't owe you
politeness or perfection-
nor to massage your male ego
while addressing female oppression.

Women don't owe you.

Women don't owe you
their virginity
or to fulfil your kink fantasy
or to get you laid-
sex is not an activity
where women replace
your masturbatory aid.

Women don't owe you.

We are born into systems
that were born before we existed
we are enlisted
as oppressor or oppressed,

and it is not anyone's fault.
But you are accountable
if you're complicit
in perpetuating the notion
that women owe you by default.

1260.

The orgasm gap
normalizes misogyny.
The gender pay gap
normalizes misogyny.
Slut shaming
normalizes misogyny.
Victim blaming
normalizes misogyny.
Patriarchy
normalizes misogyny.

It's harder to see misogyny
when we normalize misogyny.

1261.

I'm not talking you Mr. Man.
I know you don't want to hear me
(but I know you can).

I'm talking to
my mother
my sister
my daughter
my girl friend,
telling her
about the ways you oppress her
as you pretend,
that it is a natural law and order
that God has sent.

***

Patriarchy precedes religion.

It is not a coincidence
that your Holy book reeks of misogyny;
those laws didn't come from an omnipresent deity
or sent down from heaven.

Those laws were written by the men
who wanted a divine justification
for them to continue controlling women.

***

How convenient it is
for men
to use religion
to control women
and then blame it all on God.
How convenient it is
for man
to blame it all on another man
that does not exist
to be questioned.

1262.

God is not yours.

Telling you,
to tell me
what to do.

God is not yours.

Assigning sins and chores
for women like a birthright,
and when we say no
when we fight
you tell us that ain't right.

God is not yours.

When you fuck me
on all fours,
and moan the name of God
seeing nothing odd
that you call him
only when you are inside me.

God is not yours.

Can't you see?
You only call him
while you're in me.

God is in me.

1263.

"Stop speaking ill
of MY RELIGION!" they bark at me.

My religion.

But it's also *my religion.*

They say it as if religion belongs to them
and it's been hijacked by my men,
who ripped it like a beautiful flower from the soil
and tossed the petals into mud, and filth, and turmoil.

They want their words to make me recoil.

But your religion is my religion too
both of our experiences are true.
Your lived reality is not the same as mine-
because religion is a text
and text is interpreted and re-interpreted
all the time.

***

Religion is a text
and text is language
and language is subject to interpretation
and interpretation is always subjective.

***

And at some point
you need to stop praying
and start doing.

1264.

There is no such thing as
a Muslim child
a Christian child
a Jewish child
a Hindu child
a [insert religion] child.

We [insert religion] to child.

No children
are born with religion-
it is parents
who make them pick a side.

***

"You can't be friends with Jews!"
they blatantly blast.
"That's the way things are
you're better off staying far
for generations we've been at war-
this hate is passed from a past!"

And as they amassed
the grudges of ancestry
to build a future out of history,
I asked them for a logical forecast;
"So if we can't befriend one another
how much longer,

will this hate war last?"

***

I refuse to hold onto my ancestors grudges.
This generation must acknowledge,
that hate wars are a crime.
And to fight those hate wars
we must choose love over scars,
to heal all time.

1265.

"Are you an ex-Muslim?"
people often ask me,
because I loudly critique
religious cruelty.

To be honest,
I don't know whether I'm an ex-Muslim
or whether I'm even allowed to be.

Because being Muslim isn't just a religion;
it is culture, tradition,
and identity.

Can I strip from my own
blood and bone,
and still be me?

N.B. How can you leave a place that has no door?

1266.

God doesn't need messengers,
to deliver to us his words.

God speaks to us in our heads and our hearts,
in all times and all worlds.

Religion books are written by people
who want to tell people what to do.

Religion books make it easy
for people to justify their bigotry
because liberation was never the goal of religion;
those texts are written
for power, for control,
and for oppression...

***

My mother always said
she doesn't want to go to heaven.

Because heaven is made up
by the same men who made up
sexist laws and called them 'religion'.

My mother always said
she doesn't want to go to heaven.

Because she speculates that heaven

is also just another place to regulate women.

1267.

Imagine
living as a hunter-gather
in a world of gender equality.
But then settlement shifts to farming
which brings high morbidity
and high fertility,
and while you're exhausted from being pregnant and nursing sick
children
your husband says;
"Don't worry honey, I'll manage our property".

And thousands of years later
you're feeling all better,
but your husband won't share property ownership or childcare
responsibility,
and to your horror
he's built an entire system
where all men benefit from your oppression
in a new world of inequality.

Discouraging you from birth control, abortion, study, work, and the
vote
to force you
back into
childbearing and child-rearing,
blaming it all on a God that has spoken
then turning your oppressions
into laws and religions,
if you sin, you're not God-fearing.

And while you're screaming at the injustice,

men call you a "man-hater"
accusing your sanity as you being insane.
Thus upon seeing your fate,
your sisters decide to play
a different game-
they internalize and practice their misogyny
and men reward them for their pain.
But there's a fine line...
for if they bend the rules or step out of line,
they're accused of "toxic femininity"
and for this toxicity
they are to blame.

Imagine,
that this isn't fiction
or a horror tale
or a show on Broadway.

This is non-fiction;
it is the origin
and upholding of patriarchy,
as we know it today.

1268.

When we talk about the harms of patriarchy we automatically think it's just about sexism and misogyny. But that's not all.

It's true patriarchy hates women, because it only loves men. But- *not all men* are loved equally by the patriarchy.

Patriarchy has a preference, and it prefers the White, heterosexual, abled, rich, cis man. This preference is why patriarchy is also responsible for not only sexism and misogyny, but also racism, transphobia, homophobia, ableism, classism, and so many forms of modern normalized "terrorisms".

1269.

It is not a coincidence that the mantras
"not all men" and "not all cops"
take after one another-
sexism and racism
have the same father.

N.B. His name is Patriarchy.

1270.

In the slavery days
Black people weren't slaves.

They were artists
who were enslaved.
They were doctors
who were enslaved.
They were lawyers
who were enslaved.
They were engineers
who were enslaved.
They were scientists
who were enslaved.
They were architects
who were enslaved.
They were teachers
who were enslaved.
They were musicians
who were enslaved.
They were mothers and fathers
and sisters and brothers
and sons and daughters
and dreamers and lovers
who were enslaved.

In the slavery days
Black people weren't slaves.
Black people were free;
White people held them
under captivity.

N.B. Black people were **<u>not slaves</u>**. They were **<u>enslaved</u>**. Language matters.

1271.

For every Black body forced breathless
I stand as an ally screaming fearless,
yet helpless...

Helpless...

Helpless against a system making it clear
that no one can steer
away, the ships of White supremacy
sailing on oceans of Black,
stealing the breaths from the night
like the wind forced to exile the lungs
and not welcomed back.

Another murder, another injustice,
another one they want us to sit back.

I won't sit back.
I will use whatever weapon I have
my mind
my tongue
my pen-
I will fight for human rights
for each one of them.

***

Breonna.

Breonna, I'm sorry.

I'm sorry for demanding justice
from a system that isn't built for this.
What did I expect?
Their conscience would suddenly
wake up today?
When they are the ones
who proudly robbed your breath
from seeing the light of the next day...
When they instil the same fears
for over 400 years
in every Black person, every day.
I'm guilty, of foolishness
for expecting justice from criminals
who built a system to uphold their crimes.
I'm sorry, that your story
killed you, twice, in one lifetime.

Breonna, I'm sorry.

I'm sorry for demanding justice
from a system that is built-
to possibly, consider, whether
your *life matters*,
but only after
you've been killed.

N.B. Police officers have not been charged for killing Breonna Taylor. In fact one of them has a book deal.

1272.

Racial killings
are a result of
racial violence
which is a result of
racial discrimination
which is a result of
racial bullying
which is a result of
racial jokes
which is a result of
racial stereotypes
which is a result of
racism.

Racism
leads to
racial stereotypes
which leads to
racial jokes
which leads to
racial bullying
which leads to
racial discrimination
which leads to
racial violence
which leads to
racial killings.

For this racial genocide pattern to end,
we must start to see
how it all adds up in the end.

1273.

They went
from whips to bullets
and from masters to police-
Black people
cannot be free,
when countries are built
by and for
White supremacy.

***

The police consistently fail
to call out racial and misogynistic crimes,
because the police are protecting a system
that is racist and misogynistic for all time.

1274.

"The police won't shoot Black people
if they won't resist arrest!" the racists say.

"Black people won't resist arrest
if they weren't at risk of police shooting them anyway!"
I say,
"no one would logically calmly cooperate
when THEY KNOW
they are in harm's way.
Fleeing is a natural logical choice
of a survival defence mechanism
when you weigh,
the chances
that you'll die if you flee
and you'll die if you stay!"

***

I urge you to recognize that it is
a natural human response
to "fight" or "flight" the police.
Not everyone can "freeze"
in situations of fear.
Black people shouldn't die
because cops don't understand
basic physiology.

1275.

The expectations you have
of the *untrained* civilians
to not panic, stay calm, and appease-
are the expectations you should have
for the fucking *trained* police.

***

Saying
cops can kill civilians
if they won't cooperate
is like saying
doctors can kill patients
if they won't cooperate.

N.B. Qualified immunity vs. Malpractice.

1276.

Walking away from a cop
does not warrant a death sentence.

Resisting arrest
does not warrant a death sentence.

Having a past criminal record
does not warrant a death sentence.

Arresting a current criminal
does not warrant a death sentence.

Carrying a theoretical gun
does not warrant a death sentence.

Even carrying a real gun
does not warrant a death sentence.

Being Black
does not warrant a death sentence.

Being a cop
does not warrant executing a death sentence.

***

The danger is not
the Black man
who *might* have a gun
and *might* use it.

The danger is
the cop
who *actually* has a gun-
and is authorized to use it
without repercussion.

1277.

When a Black person
is shot by the police,
their past criminal record
is pulled up
as if to justify
the current (unrelated) shooting.
But what we need to know
is the past criminal record
of the police,
and how often they got away
with anti-Black racism
with no prosecuting.

**

Instead of the Black man's
past criminal records
making headline-
I want to see the cop's
past police brutality record
making headline.

Shift the focus from victim
to the perpetrator of the crime.

Instead of showing
the criminal record
of the Black man shot,
show us the anti-Black racist record

of the cop doing the shooting-
because far too many cops are getting away with this
without prosecuting.

A Black person doesn't owe cops
good behaviour
for the human right to live-
but cops owe Black people
good behaviour,
to protect and serve with that badge
not to murder with!

N.B. Any news article that shows you the criminal record of the
victim shot by the cops, is attempting to derail your attention and
justify the shooting by victim blaming.

1278.

"He is a sex addict
who just had a bad day,
it's not racially motivated",
that's what the police have to say.

And I wonder if they realize the dismay?

For their micro-aggression in language
followed by gaslighting silence,
IS the White supremacy that leads to
misogyny
victim-blaming sex workers
and anti-Asian violence.

N.B. On March 16th, 2021, Robert Aaron Long killed 8 people (6 of whom were Asian women) in a mass shooting spree in which he targeted Asian spa and massage parlours in Atlanta U.S.A. because he "wanted to rid himself of sexual temptation". Police later claimed "he was just having a bad day".

1279.

White supremacy
is above the law;
because
White supremacists
created the law.

***

Laws are language.
Regulations are language.

The misogyny, homophobia, and racism
in laws and regulations
is language.

For change
we just need to change
the language.

1280.

We are a world that controls
the wrong controls.

We control wombs
instead of guns.

We control how girls dress
instead of educate our sons.

We control freedom
instead of impunity.

We control only what keeps us
controlled by the patriarchy.

N.B. According to Amnesty International, more than 500 people die
every day from gun violence, and an estimated 2,000 people are
injured by gunshots every single day. Gun violence disproportionately
impacts communities of colour, women and other marginalized
groups in society.

1281.

How can you expect justice
from a system built by your oppressor?
How can you expect lawful protection
from laws written to benefit your aggressor?

To have justice, to be protected,
and to have a world built
upon fairness-
you must change the backward mindset
passed on from generation to the next
without any awareness.

It starts with you.

How are you reflecting?
And what are you teaching
your kids too?

N.B. We need to start *somewhere* to get *there*.

1282.

Goldilocks and the Three Bears
is a story about colonialism
and White privilege.
A White girl feels entitled
to enter a native's home which
she calmly invades,
and not only
does she have the audacity
to help herself to their stuff,
but also to rest in their beds
not worried about being caught
or scolded off.

Goldilocks
is the Karen of Karen.

***

"Ken" and "Karen"
barged into heaven
taking front-row seats on Judgement Day.

God told them those seats are given
to those who combat privilege and racism-
so they asked to speak to the manager right away!

***

Calling out
White supremacy
is not an attack on White people-
and as a White person if you feel calling it out is an attack
then you recognize that you are benefiting
from White supremacy covering your back.

And you don't want to end that.

1283.

Grumpy.
Dopey.
Doc.
Happy.
Bashful.
Sneezy.
Sleepy.

The names of the seven dwarfs
actually represent,
the outcome of male privilege
and entitlement.

While *Snow White*
is the embodiment,
of White privilege
in White feminism.

How else can you explain
a woman being safe living with seven strange men?

She benefits from her proximity to them.

She is willing to see other women
as the enemy,
and serve the seven men in exchange for some
pseudo protection in their patriarchy.

For her evil stepmother is only evil
because she no longer follows

the patriarchal standards of beauty.

Snow White won't do that,
she has internalized her misogyny-
she complies to standards of beauty
and serves men like it's her duty.

1284.

Perhaps she's just a shitty person
and it's not White supremacy.

Perhaps he pulled the 'race card'
and her attack on him
wasn't motivated racially.

Or perhaps,
White supremacy enables her shitty behaviour-
and he pulled the 'race card'
because in her fucked up game
that's the only card dealt to him as a waiver.

***

They say;
It's not about race!
The cops are killing White people too!

I say;
So why the fuck then
aren't you demanding
to defund the police, too???
Or are you willing to sacrifice
a few White lives
just to keep
your racism alive?!

This is the classic demonstration, if only we realize,
of the danger of White folks who uphold White supremacy
(or any folks who uphold their extremist oppressive ideology);
they are willing to kill their own folk
just to maintain superiority.

N.B. Muslim terrorists also kill other Muslims.

1285.

If you are justifying
why Black people
are shot by cops-
you are defending
cops for shooting
Black people.

And if you are defending
cops for shooting
Black people-
then you defend
cops to shoot
all people...

Because ALL LIVES MATTER equally, right?

***

Perhaps the *Titanic* couldn't be saved
because as it hit the iceberg and the captain called for help
the response was:
ALL SHIPS MATTER!

1286.

Throughout history,
every White man I learned about
is represented as someone
who has done something
great,
and yet every Black man I learned about
has actually done something
to liberate himself
from the evils of the White man.

Perhaps the White man
is not as great
as he wants history to believe.
Perhaps the White man
is only great
when it comes to deceive.

***

Trump is the best president for America.

America wasn't discovered by Columbus.

You can't discover a country
that is already
discovered.

In writing history
let's *right* history,

this is the real story;

America was stolen by Columbus.

America was stolen
from Indigenous people,
and built each brick
from the backbones
of enslaved Africans.
Did your school teach you
about the *real* Americans?

They tore the skin off Black backs
tossed them at 400 years of setbacks.
They're killed, to be free
in a world continually constructed
to criminalize the Black body.
Did your school teach you
who's *really* guilty?

White supremacy is not so complicated;
they rip the shirt off your back
and then they scold you for being naked.

America is the land of the free
Indigenous people.
America is the home of the brave
Black people.

Isn't it ironic that the *American Dream*
is to get a job and a home?
This land continues to yearn
for what it knows

it never earned
with its blood and bone.

To truly *Make America Great Again*,
this country must acknowledge
and repay history.
But Trump is the best president for America,
if the plan is to keep building
a future out of misery.

N.B. Vote. In writing the future, right the history.

1287.

They ask why I,
as an Arab woman,
who lives in the Middle East
cares who wins
the U.S. elections?

America is my cool Aunt.

America is where I go
to wear whatever I want,
to strip off my hijab
and to proudly flaunt
my ideas and my mind-
America is where I go
to find my kind
of humankind.

America is my cool Aunt.

America is where I go
when my Mother
doesn't let me go
out, with that boy I like.
America is where I go
when I want to kiss another girl
and won't get killed
for being labelled a 'dyke'.

America is where I go
to party, to work,
to study, to read,

to be human
in a world that needs
humanity.

America is where I go
to let go
of the sacred
and embrace the profanity.

America is where I go
to make mistakes,
and to have fun on spring breaks.
To not worry about the stakes
of skinny dipping on a sunny day,
to be invincible and invisible-
because no one knows my name
or asks what my father will say.

Everyone's business
is to mind their own business-
in America God doesn't tell men
to tell me how to pray.

America is where I go
when I want to get drunk
on life, on love.
America is where I go
when I've had enough.

America is where I go
when my body is unwell,
to heal, to feel,
my heartbeats swell.

America is where
my best friend got
a safe abortion.
America is where
my brother is living safely
without religious devotion.

America is my cool Aunt.

America is where I go
to be on my best
bad behaviour,
because America is where
I am allowed
to be my own saviour.

It is the land of the free
and the brave
and the raves
and of apple pies,
and of people who aren't afraid
to call out racism, hypocrisy, misogyny, homophobia, and lies.
It is where to keep freedom of speech alive
everything else dies.

I'm not saying that America is perfect
but it is the next best thing-
for an Arab woman deprived
of what it means to be a human being.

That is why I,
as an Arab woman,
who lives in the Middle East
cares who wins
the U.S. elections.

America is my cool Aunt.

Who doesn't care if their cool Aunt
marries a racist, sexist,
homophobic, misogynist,
fool?

I care, because America is my cool Aunt
and I want her to stay cool.

1288.

We're all racists.

If you're not a racist,
you've enabled racism.
If you haven't enabled it,
you've ignored it.
If you haven't ignored it,
you've been silent about it.

And saying "no, not me",
is a way of holding on
to privilege,
by letting go
of responsibility.

We're all guilty.

All equations, add up equally
and the current equation is this:

So many Black people are struggling
in the world as it is,
because *so many non-Black people*
aren't actively
anti-racist.

***

To end racism
it is not enough
to fight racism.

You need to hate racism.

You need to hate racism,
the way racism hates Black people.

You need to be racist
towards racism.

***

It is important
that we see colour
that we acknowledge racism
that we acknowledge it exists.

And it is equally important
that we do not see colour
that we acknowledge we are all equal to one another
that we acknowledge we must be anti-racist.

To be anti-racist,
we must see race.
To not be racist
we must not see race.

1289.

"Black folks have privilege too-
they're getting more job opportunities than me,
because companies now want diversity!"
cried the White man.

He doesn't seem to understand
that giving space for Black folks
is not a privilege
but a right they have been denied
for oh so many years.

He's not used to seeing Black folks get
what he normally gets-
equality, to the oppressor, is one of his worst fears.

                              ***

White folks created the N word.
Black folks have taken and reclaimed it.
Now White folks are upset
because they aren't allowed to use it.

A word.

White folks; you're upset over a fucking insult of a word
that Black folks reclaimed from you-
when you have stolen their sweat and blood,
and the backbones that hold their future too.

Privilege is when you cannot see,
that your feelings being hurt
is not the same
as the pain
experienced by someone's lived reality.

You stole
Black music
Black hair
Black art
Black everything
and appropriated it-
now you're upset over an insult
that Black folks reclaimed?

1290.

Is it
grey or gray?
Colour or color?

And why does it matter,
which spelling I use
British or American
or whether I am consistent?

English
isn't my mother's womb anyway,
but the world has been persistent
in spoon feeding it to my tongue
whenever I'm hungry to learn...

They ignore that I'm starving
for the Arabic I inherited
from my mother's flesh
and my father's sperm.

1291.

Celebrating Christmas
as a non-Christian
and I wonder
whether it's
appropriation
or commercialization
or internalization
or indoctrination
or Westernization
or simply
just a sparkly
fascination?

Perhaps it's all of the above
because it's the aftermath
of colonization.

***

Cultural appropriation
is going to dine in a fancy Indian cuisine
when you just condemned your Indian neighbour,
for the abhorrent scent of their cooking
filling the apartment building's corridor.

1292.

I look at the box
that says
'alien'.

My mother tells me
to tick it.

"But Mama", I say
"I am human.
And no human
is an alien".

                              ***

I am not a refugee;
this earth doesn't belong to you
nor does it belong
to me.

This earth was born
free;
just like you
and me.

1293.

There's a public football field
in our neighbourhood
where teen boys would always be playing
dressed in nothing
but shorts,
enjoying
the air on their skin
and the activity of sports.

I never saw girls play.
There is no law against that, so to say.

And it's not that this is a "boy's game"
and girls don't want to play it.
What's happening is the classic display
of male privilege.
Girls cannot play sports publically
without boys ogling at their bodies
and perhaps harassing them.

So when we fight
for our girls and women's rights,
we don't just want to be incorporated
into laws that are equal for all,
we also want to change mindsets
that stop us from safely
play ball.

1294.

Outside the train station
in London's underground,
a man pulled out his penis
and pissed on public ground.

I stopped in my tracks astonished
(not by the sight or the sound),
but by the fact that he felt completely *safe*
not just to pee in the street,
but to expose his meat.

No worries about anyone
sexualizing him
or assaulting him
or getting him beat.

And here I was wearing
just a slightly short skirt
showing just some thigh skin
(not my genitals for all to see);
but I was still scared
of what could go wrong
when men gaze at me.

1295.

When non-men are treated equally to men
you can say *I don't see gender*.

When non-Whites are treated equally to Whites
you can say *I don't see race*.

But when injustice and inequality
is unshakably in place
based on gender and race,
not seeing gender and race
means that you don't see
that injustice and inequality.
And you can't fix what you can't see
thus oppression will continue to be,
harming us based on gender and race.

You have to see, to fix- you can't just jump to erase.

1296.

Of course you don't realize your privilege!

You don't realize your privilege
because you are accustomed to it
like the way you don't realize
how you take each breath
gulping that air,
trusting that the next dose
will just be there.

Hold your nose.
Close your mouth.

Stop breathing-
see how long you can last.
Reflect on what you take for granted
in your future and past.

Realize that there is
enough air to sustain us all.
Use your privilege
to give,
not to control.

***

Privilege is like having an airbag in your car;
it's there to protect you-

even if you're not using it,
even if you can't see it at all times,
and even if you're the one
who caused hurt onto others.

Telling you to check your privilege
is not blaming you for having an airbag in your car-
it is to acknowledge that there are people walking on the street
with their two feet,
and they don't have any airbags or a car.
If you don't see them, you'll crash into them
you can kill them, without causing yourself so much as a scar.

***

Privilege does not
discriminate between
those it privileges.

Nor does oppression.

1297.

You can't strip off your privilege like a piece of clothing at the end of the day. But that doesn't mean there's nothing you can do about it either.

It is important to take time to understand your privilege because this is where you hold power.

Understanding your power will help you use it for good. It will help you see how you benefit from your privilege (whether intentionally or unintentionally) at the expense of others. It will help you fight for (and with) others who are paying their lives because of a system of privilege created by our ancestors (and maintained by us), without any logic and with no purpose other than benefiting some people through harming others by holding power over them.

We can dismantle this system. We should dismantle this system because this world belongs to all of us, equally. Dismantling starts with being aware of your privileges. Let your defence mode rest, strip off the discomfort that comes with acknowledging truth, and tell yourself honestly;

What are your privileges?

***

You know why even the privileged
should dismantle systems of privilege?

Because privilege

isn't handed to anyone for free;
you need to pay a certain price to uphold it
and it dictates how much that price will be.

Reflect on your privileges. And you will see.

How much are you willing to pay
to be free?

1298.

"You have privilege
you're the daughter of a king",
they say.

That privilege is why
I am not allowed
to see the light of day.

That privilege is why
I am not allowed
to speak what my mind wants to say.

That privilege is why
each step of mine is measured
based on what people would say.

That privilege is why
I must follow the protocols
and never have my own way.

That privilege is why
I only exist in pictures you see in the news
but never in person, never in your shoes,
because I am hidden away.

That privilege is why
you never run into me in the corner store
or down the neighbourhood,
or even spot me on a deserted highway.

That privilege is why

I am oppressed
every day.

N.B. Princess Latifa of U.A.E is imprisoned in her father's palace
after attempting to escape the country. In other news, Meghan Markle
comes forward to speak about the oppression in the palace.

1299.

"Oh look at Meghan Markle crying about oppression,
while she lived in a palace like a princess!" they say.

Hello, this might come as a shock;
racial privilege isn't afforded to you, by fortune or by luck.

No matter how rich one is-
no money can "purchase" racial privilege,
so don't confuse the privilege of being rich
with skin colour privilege.

And if a Duchess has it that bad
just imagine what ordinary
Black folks experience daily.

1300.

Patriarchal ladder: Rungs of privilege.

Race: Whites on top

_____

Class: Rich on top

_____

Sex: males on top

_____

Gender: men on top

_____

Sexuality: heterosexual on top

_____

Body: abled on top

_____

If you're a white, rich, male, cis, who is heterosexual and abled- you attain the highest benefits from patriarchy.

What step are you on, on the patriarchal ladder?

Draw out your rungs. Reflect on your privilege.

1301.

You see
how beautifully
the ocean
intersects
with the sky and the sand?

Intersectional feminism
is just like that-
you have to see the full picture,
in order to understand.

***

Think of intersectional feminism
as this huge massive pie,
and the layers inside
are made of
race, class, sex, gender
and whatnot.

You can't take a bite of a layer
and claim you've tried the entire pie.

You can't claim to be a feminist
if you don't fight for you, and them, and I.

1302.

Privilege is like Lego pieces;
when you put different parts together
you build different paths all together.

A Black piece on its own
has no power-
but if you fix it with
man, cis, heterosexual, abled, and rich pieces
you begin to have a tower.

A White piece on its own
holds all power-
but if you fix it with
woman, trans, homosexual, disabled, and poor pieces
you begin to dismantle the tower.

I am a Brown Lego piece
and assigned as a female,
if you put those two together
the privilege engine is a fail-
but if you add that I'm cis, heterosexual, abled, and rich
in many situations
I can easily reach the holy grail.

Reflect on your Lego pieces
what do they entail?

Unless you're a male
who is also White, cis, heterosexual, abled, and rich
(i.e. you've hit the jackpot of privilege);
privilege and oppression

are the two sides of everyone's tale.

***

A cis White heterosexual rich abled man
has privilege over
a cis White heterosexual rich abled woman.

A cis White heterosexual rich abled woman
has privilege over
a cis Black heterosexual rich abled man.

A cis Black heterosexual rich abled man
has privilege over
a cis Black heterosexual rich abled woman.

A cis Black heterosexual rich abled woman
has privilege over
a trans Black heterosexual rich abled woman.

A trans Black heterosexual rich abled woman
has privilege over…
(and it just keeps going).

1303.

We all hold privileges and oppressions,
like grudges and heirlooms.

We pass them on to our children,
and that's how they linger and loom.

And bloom.

So check yourself.
Reflect. Dissect.

Be aware of the way you move in the world.
Be aware of the voices you silence when they need be heard.

This is the way to make the world,
a better place for all.
This is the way to make our limited time here,
a pleasant stroll.

1304.

"Why should I hold any accountability?
It's not my fault that I was born
a White or a male or a heterosexual
in this patriarchy!"
he says,
claiming victimhood on top of privilege,
having it all
and totally oblivious.

"No one said it's your fault"
I tell him
"We are all born into different systems
that existed before us as a default.
But there is one way we all have equality
and that's in the fact that we all
have a responsibility
and a moral duty
not just to live and venture,
but to leave this world
better than when we entered".

***

Being a woman
is not a choice,
but being a misogynist
is a choice.

Being Black
is not a choice,

but being a racist
is a choice.

Being homosexual
is not a choice,
but being a homophobic
is a choice.

Being privileged
is not a choice,
but how you use your privilege
is always a choice.

1305.

"NOT ALL MEN"
he yells again,
"I am a man and I have never caused
a woman pain!
Stop making assumptions that ALL MEN
are the same!"

His logic is akin
to a Black person
oppressed for their skin,
and calling out White supremacy
and the response from a White person would be;
"but I'm a White person who never hurt anyone so don't blame me".

There are good white people, but ALL white people have racial
privilege.
Just like there are good men, but ALL men have gender privilege.

The world is safer for you, as a man, than it is for me as a woman.
The world protects your crimes against me (should you decide to
commit them), justifies them, and lets you get away with them.

If this pure fact hurts your feelings,
imagine how women feel to know
that your main concern is your ego
and you don't want to realize;
that our concerns are not a broken heart
but the lack of safety we face
our entire lives.

And let me tell you this;

putting your ego over our actual fears
is yet actually in itself
another example
of your gender privilege.

***

The problem of the privileged
is not their privilege;
it's when they refuse
to acknowledge
their privilege.

1306.

Not all White people
uphold White supremacy;
but White supremacy
upholds all White people.

Not all cis men
uphold patriarchy;
but patriarchy
upholds all cis men.

Not all heterosexuals
uphold heteronormativity;
but heteronormativity
upholds all heterosexuals.

Not all abled
uphold ableism;
but ableism
upholds all abled.

Not all the rich
uphold classism;
but classism
upholds all the rich.

Not all the privileged
uphold systems of oppression;
but systems of oppression
are upheld
by the silence of those it privileges.

1307.

The refusal
to acknowledge
one's privilege
is not purely naivety;
it is, in itself, an acknowledgement
of one's resistance
to accountability.
It is how the privileged
maintain privilege
in its entirety.

The men
who act all attacked
when asked
to check their privilege,
are deflecting
simply because
they're not wanting
to give up their privilege.

***

I think
even
when
cis men
are not aware of the patriarchy
as an insidious system,

it is impossible they are not aware
of how their gender affords them privilege at the expense of others.

They either stop to think how to use that privilege for the greater good
OR continue to reap benefits and not give a fuck how they hurt others.
They have a choice, and the ones who are choosing to hurt others
know exactly what they're doing.

And when they act
all attacked
when you point out their privilege
this is a big red flag
that they KNOW exactly how they are reaping benefits
and don't want to be made uncomfortable for doing so.

Denial of privilege
is, in itself, a privilege.

1308.

It's not that
men don't know any better-
it's that they're allowed
to not know any better.

Perhaps it's true- 'boys will be boys'
because only men can be feminists.

***

If 'boys
will be
boys',
then girls
must be
feminists.

Because we sure as fuck
won't be their victims.

***

The problem is
we think of privilege
like a pie;
the more others take
the less left for you.
But that's not true.

We should think of privilege
like a candle;
lighting another candle
does not dim yours.

1309.

Having privilege
does not mean
you have no hardships.
It means your privilege
is not the cause
of your hardships.

***

White privilege doesn't mean
that White people don't struggle;
it means that their struggles
aren't because of their skin colour.

Male privilege doesn't mean
that males don't struggle;
it means that their struggles
aren't because of their sex.

Cis privilege doesn't mean
that cis people don't struggle;
it means that their struggles
aren't because of their gender.

Heterosexual privilege doesn't mean
that heterosexuals don't struggle;
it means that their struggles
aren't because of their sexual orientation.

Abled privilege doesn't mean

that abled people don't struggle;
it means that their struggles
aren't because of their ability.

Rich privilege doesn't mean
that rich people don't struggle;
it means that their struggles
aren't because of their financial status.

Having privilege doesn't mean
that privileged people don't struggle;
it means that their struggles
aren't because of their privilege.

1310.

Having privilege
is like having Coronavirus;
you may not realize your symptoms
but it doesn't mean you won't hurt others.

***

You can never understand
the oppressions that
others experience for your privilege to be maintained,
unless you understand
the privileges that
you experience at their expense.

When you do not see
your privilege,
you cannot see
the oppression.

1311.

We refer to
a White friend as a friend
but a Black friend as a *Black* friend.

We refer to
a male athlete as an athlete
but a female athlete as a *female* athlete.

We refer to
a heterosexual colleague as a colleague
but a gay colleague as a *gay* colleague.

A cis activist is an activist
but a trans activist is a *trans* activist.

An abled artist is an artist
but a disabled artist is a *disabled* artist.

Privilege gives the privileged
a cloak of invisibility,
while oppression
is the core of a marginalized identity.

Perhaps that's why checking one's privilege isn't easy
but identifying oppression is breezy.

Marginalization is central to the identity of the oppressed.

1312.

Our work is not done
by just voting.
We must keep on
dismantling
the toxic systems
we're upholding.

ALL of those who are
in any way privileged,
(even those who aren't actively pursuing
that privilege for themselves)-
have a responsibility to dismantle
the systems that uphold them,
at the expense of everyone else.

It doesn't matter
that not all White people are the same
not all cops are the same
not all men are the same-
what matters is
that White supremacy
the policing strategy
and misogyny
are a fucking pain
for all of modern society.

1313.

ALL WHITE PEOPLE
benefit from White supremacy.

ALL CIS MEN
benefit from patriarchy.

ALL HETEROSEXUALS
benefit from heteronormativity.

ALL ABLED
benefit from ableism.

ALL RICH PEOPLE
benefit from classism.

So when the oppressed call you out
don't gaslight
by saying shit like;
"no not me",
"not all men",
"all lives matter".
Instead listen, reflect, and ask;
"how can I make this sick world
a little bit better?"

Because that's how we make
this sick world
a whole lot better.

1314.

"Why is it okay
for women to call men trash,
but if men did the same
they get a strong backlash?!"
he exclaimed!

So, again, I fucking explained;
"Because we merely *call you* trash
and you complain
that it's upsetting,
but you *treat us* like trash
and except us
to say and do nothing!
And before you say women can treat men like trash too-
do some research to see that this isn't systemic or institutionalized,
yet look at all the countries
that *still* practice
female infanticide and femicide,
and honour killings-
if this is a competition,
women aren't winning.
Look at the rates of intimate partner violence
and when women speak out from silence,
you accuse us of lying.
You're butt hurt when *our tongues* say 'men are trash'
yet with *your hands* women are dying!"

***

"Imagine if men say that to you!
What would you do?"
he snaps offended, when I dare
to speak of men in the same way
that they always snare
at me.

"I don't need to imagine
this is my lived reality"
I tell him,
"this is the norm in society,
this is what I hear daily
and I'm expected to shut up
while eating your shit as naturally true-
you tell me, why are you offended to imagine
what you do to women
to be inflicted on you?"

1315.

Imagine if I talk about men
the way they talk about women.

Imagine if I reduce them
to the status of their virginity;
convince them that their natural
sexual desire
is a sign of them being slutty.

Imagine if I say I prefer men
the way I prefer my tampon;
sealed, clean,
never been
inside anyone.

Imagine that this is taught as part of sex education for everyone.

Imagine if I tell men
their dicks are just like erasers,
they get shorter and shorter
each time they have sex-
and that they are whores if they don't
save themselves.

Imagine.

Imagine if I judge a man
based on nothing other than his looks,
how well he cleans, how well he cooks.
Imagine if I tell him there's no need
to aspire to anything in life,

because let's not pretend-
that his greatest achievement is
anything other than
being a husband.

Imagine.

Imagine we flip the double standards
like pancakes in a pan-
how will it feel
to be a man?

***

The only way men can
truly experience reverse sexism,
is if we reverse *time*
and put them under our oppression.

N.B. Reverse sexism doesn't exist.

1316.

Have you realized why
White people shout "all lives matter"
at Black Lives Matter events,
men accuse all feminists
of hating men,
and heterosexuals whine
about not having a Pride Day for them?

They do that because they are afraid
of the tables turning against them.

If you have this irrational fear
in your mind
of "reverse oppression"-
it means you know for sure
that you're treating "others"
with aggression.

***

Oppressors cannot understand, believe, or imagine,
the concept of equality
because that's not the reality
of how they've been running the world.

If they don't want you to be equal to them
they're benefiting from your oppression then.

1317.

There is no such thing as
reverse sexism
reverse racism
heterophobia
cisphobia.

Oppressors who try to claim
the rallying cries of oppression;
do so to remain
at the centre of the conversation.

***

Men who interrupt feminists
to say "you hate men",
are just trying
to re-centre themselves
into the conversation.

White supremacists who interrupt Black Lives Matter
to say "all lives matter",
are just trying
to re-centre themselves
into the conversation.

Heterosexuals who interrupt the LGBTQI+ community
to say "we need straight pride",
are just trying
to re-centre themselves

into the conversation.

It is not a coincidence, that there is a pattern;
oppressors don't want our love
they don't even want to be a part of
a constructive conversation.
All they want to do
is to
distract and disrupt our activism
by re-centring themselves
into the conversation.

1318.

Men
who, when called out
for being hostile,
become hostile-
are simply proving
that they are in fact
hostile.

Abusers who claim victimhood
are simply derailing the conversation
to make themselves the focus again.
That is the problem with abusers- they want to be at the focus and
willing to pay any price for that (even if it means playing victim).

***

Learn to recognize some of the common ways in which men centre
themselves to stifle feminist discourse;

What they say:
1- Not all men! You can't generalize!
2- All feminists hate men! (Yes I can generalize!)
3- Feminism is no longer needed because I would never hurt a
woman. I help women. I don't know any man who hurts women.
4- I don't hate women because I have a mother/sister/wife/daughter.
5- What about male victims?

How it shifts focus away from the topic discussed:
1- Redirects your focus to explain that you don't believe all men are

guilty.

2- Redirects your focus to explain that not all feminists hate men.

3- Redirects your attention to himself- as if he represents ALL MEN (which is pretty ironic especially when he spent time proving why NOT ALL MEN are the same).

4- Assumes his proximity to other women makes him non-predatory. Again we are talking about him. And it's fucking irrelevant- women are often hurt by the men they know and trust.

5- Redirects your attention from female victims to male victims (it's important to note that ALL victims are valid, but when the only time male victims are brought up is when the discussion is about female victims it becomes akin to the "all lives matter" argument).

1319.

When you attack homosexuality
you also support homophobia.

When you attack feminism
you also support misogyny.

When you attack Black Lives Matter
you also support White supremacy.

When you blame rape victims
you also excuse rapists.

Who are you defending?
What are you permitting?

It matters what we speak,
so let's speak about what matters.

1320.

Men who are misogynists
and White supremacists
have been playing the
'gender/race card'
to get ahead
for so long-
and then they dare accuse the oppressed
of using the 'gender/race card'
when the oppressed don't play along!

***

White supremacists
get really pissed
when they're convinced
that Black, Indigenous,
and People of Colour,
are using the 'race card'
because that's
their card!

And men who are misogynists
get really pissed
when they're convinced
that women
are using the 'gender card'
because that's
their card!

Farida D.

BIPOC's and Women;
stick to the cards in your lane!
Can't you see- it's not fun
when you mess up
the rules of the game?!

1321.

The "All Lives Matter", "Not All Men", and "Straight Pride" dudes
walked into a bar.

They were all eyeing a Black woman
who was sitting afar.

The "All Lives Matter" said he'll approach her first,
he'd date Black women because he wasn't a racist.

"Hi, I'm All Lives Matter" he amplified.
"And I'm Black Lives Matter" she replied.
"So you mean MY LIFE DOESN'T MATTER?" he suddenly blew up
with rage.
"Here I am trying to be nice,
yet you're holding against me my ancestors' vice,
when THE FUCK WILL YOU TURN A NEW PAGE?????"

She ended any further attempt to engage.

So the "Not All Men" guy went next.

He said "Hi, I'm sorry about my friend- my name is Not All Men"
She told him "And I'm a lesbian".
But that didn't turn him off
as he cut her off,
"Can I try to change your mind?
You see I'm not like all men
I don't mind dating a lesbian,
in fact I can watch you have sex with other woman
I totally won't mind!"

He kept persisting, even when she politely declined;
"But how do you know that you don't like dick if you haven't even
tried?" he tried.
So she replied,
"How do you know you that you don't like dick if you haven't even
tried?"

At this point the "Straight Pride"
dude walks over,
not even the slightest bit sober.

"Hi, my name is Straight Pride" he said.
She scoffed "I already told your friend I'm not straight"-
"Oh I know" he began to taunt,
"I'm not here to ask you on a date,
I just want to flaunt
that my sexual orientation
has never gotten any hate!"

Then all the dudes laughed and laughed
and stayed up all night at the bar
drinking and having fun
and harassing more women.
For, as men, they will never know the danger
in getting drunk or walking home late-
in fact those things are used as excuses
to not hold them accountable for their mistakes.

1322.

Women *are* oppressed
because they are attacked by men.
While men *feel* attacked
when told not to oppress women.

Black folks *are* oppressed
because they are attacked by Whites.
While Whites *feel* attacked
when told not to oppress Black folks.

Queer folks *are* oppressed
because they are attacked by heterosexuals.
While heterosexuals *feel* attacked
when told not to oppress queer folks.

Marginalized folks *are* actually oppressed
while the majority folks *feel* attacked-
and because they're the majority
their feelings hold more superiority
than the actual lived pain of the minority.

Marginalized folks *are* actually oppressed
while the majority folks *feel* attacked-
and their feelings are what keep
marginalized oppression intact.

1323.

White folks
must advocate
for Black liberation-
because they enslaved and suppressed
Black folks and they need to fix the shit they've done.
It's the same with men-
they must advocate for feminism
in order to help free women.

***

As a feminist,
I don't want to put men
in my shoes.
I want to throw out
the shoes
that men put me in.

If you think feminism
wants women to
"take over",
you are admitting
women are
"taken over".

If you are worried that
feminism wants women
to be superior over men-

you are admitting
women are currently
inferior to men.

Feminism is a fight
for equality,
not for revenge.
And the man who can't see that
has done women so wrong,
he can't believe
we won't avenge.

1324.

Yes, feminism hurts men.

They won't be able
to catcall and harass
without consequence,
they won't be able
to get away with the rape
that they call "sex".
They won't get all the orgasms
without sharing.
They won't get a higher wage
or leave the dirty dishes
by the sink.
And let that sink;
they won't 'have it all'
a career and a family-
without doing it all
i.e. sharing responsibility.

Yes, feminism hurts men.
But it will only hurt
the men who'd like to continue
with hurting women.

***

If you're worried
that your feminism
would put off men,

179

darling-
you're right.
It will put off men.
But it will only put off
the men that
shouldn't stay put
in your life.

So let your feminism be your guide.

Because feminism
only feels like terrorism
to the men who benefit
from women's oppression.

And to be real-
that's exactly
how it should feel.

1325.

Dear Men,
Do you realize that we just want
to love you?
To have mutual pleasure with you?
To mutually raise a family?
And if we don't want to love you
or have sex, or a family with you
(just like some of you don't)-
we just want to be
mutually free?

Do you realize what it means
when we say we want equality?

It's mutuality.

***

If you get your power
by putting me on a leash,
then, of course, my freedom
scares you.

1326.

If calling out misogyny
makes me a man-hater,
then so be it.

If calling out White supremacy
gets me accused of using the "race card",
then so be it.

If calling out homophobia
means I'll burn in hell,
then so be it.

If I'm the bad person
for stopping bad people
from continuing to do bad things,
then so be fucking it.

***

Pro-women IS NOT anti-men.
Pro-Black IS NOT anti-White.
Pro-LGBTQI+ IS NOT anti-heterosexual.

Pro-women IS anti-patriarchy.
Pro-Black IS anti-White supremacy.
Pro- LGBTQI+ IS anti-heteronormativity.

But if you are
a White heterosexual man

who wants to uphold
patriarchy
White supremacy
and heteonormativity...

Then yes,
we are anti- you.

1327.

Women aren't perfect;
we can be horrible
we can cause trouble
we can fight
we're not always right.

Women aren't perfect,
do you know why?
Because women are human,
(just like men),
from the same dust we are born
and under it we die.

***

We talk about "mean girls"
but we never talk about "mean boys".

"Mean girls"
as a syndrome
implies that girls aren't naturally capable of being mean
thus when they are, it's shocking
and so they deserve
whatever is dealt to them
by the patriarchy.

But the oppressed do not owe the world perfection
for the basic human right of equality.

***

Abusive people exist in every gender;
abuse is not a gender trait,
but a harmful human character.

Using abusive women as an excuse to not support feminism
or Black crime to not fight against racism
means you expect perfection
from the oppressed-
you want to hold them to a higher standard first
in order to justify their humanity
otherwise they deserve their oppression.

We don't owe you perfection.
We are human. We are good and bad.
I don't have to be on my best behaviour
so that you justify not killing me as a waiver.

I don't owe you perfection
remember this;
You have no right to oppress me
no matter what my behaviour is.

The oppressed
don't owe the world
perfection.
Being 'perfect' or the 'model minority'
is not a mortgage
that the oppressed have to pay
to own the right to equality.

I don't have to be 'perfect'
for you to justify your allyship.

1328.

Should I be an ally?
When there's;
-Black on Black crime
-People of Colour hating one another
-Muslim men oppressing Muslim women
-Internalized antisemitism
-Trans people who are homophobic
-Women who uphold patriarchy

Yes, you should still be an ally!

Don't put conditions on your allyship-
and for fuck's sake
don't expect to be paid
for your allyship, with good behaviour!
Recognize that
good people and bad people
exist in every race, religion, and gender!

Why do we hold the oppressed to standards
not expected of the oppressor?!

***

Part of upholding patriarchy
is by holding
all oppressed groups
accountable to higher moral standards-
otherwise,
they deserve their oppression

and deserve to be slandered.

No Black people can be criminals,
or else all Black people
deserve to have their necks squeezed.

No women can be liars,
or else all women
deserve to be raped and not believed.

Why can't we realize
that oppressed minorities are as human
as their oppressors too?
There are good people and bad people
in every race, gender, and community.

The devil has no immunity.

Yet crimes committed by the oppressed minority
of Black people and women
and Asians
and Muslims and Jews
are used an excuse
to justify and uphold
a patriarchal, misogynist,
White supremacist
system of abuse.

And the irony of holding the crimes of the oppressed as a means to justify
the further oppressing and dividing
of people into a hierarchy-

is that the oppressed
commit their crimes in the first place
because of the oppressions of this patriarchy!

1329.

You don't get to put conditions
to decide
when it is valid to get an abortion.

You don't get to put conditions
to decide
which Black lives matter.

You don't get to put conditions
to decide
for which lives we must fight.

You don't get to put conditions
to decide
who deserves basic human rights.

***

I am not pro-hijab.
I am pro-choices.

I am not pro-mini-skirts.
I am pro-choices.

I am not pro-makeup.
I am pro-choices.

I am not pro-oppression.

I am pro-choices.

***

I don't support the porn industry
but I support people
who consent to work in porn.

I don't support the beauty industry
but I support people
who consent to use beauty products.

I don't support the hijab ideology
but I support people
who consent to wear hijab.

I don't support the concept of marriage
but I support people
who consent to getting married.

I don't support oppression;
this means I must support people
who consent to the choices they make
even if I, personally,
would choose differently.

1330.

Legalizing abortion
will not increase
the abortion rate.
It will decrease
the death rate
of women.

Because abortions are happening anyway.

Legalizing sex education
will not increase
the rate of premarital sex.
It will decrease
the rate of unsafe sex.

Because premarital sex is happening anyway.

Legalizing premarital relationships
will not increase
the rate of premarital relationships.
It will decrease
the rate of danger on the lives of women.

Because premarital relationships are happening anyway.

***

Did you know that
there are many Muslim countries
where premarital relationships are illegal?

The cost of this that women end up paying,
is fucking lethal.

Criminalizing premarital relationships
is thought to eliminate such encounters.
But legalizing premarital relationships
will not increase
the rate of premarital relationships.
It will decrease
the rate of danger on the lives of women.

Because premarital relationships are happening anyway.

But when you criminalize them,
you make the only way
to safely date
is to do it behind closed doors.
This reality,
literally
opens the doors
for rapists and abusers to get away
with their crime,
being unreported, serving no time.
Because if dating itself is a crime and done secretly
rapists and abusers are more likely
to be in a secluded safe place,
where there are no witnesses
other than the victims they deface.
And those victims (without a doubt)

won't report or speak out or shout out
because if they do
they would expose that they are "guilty" for dating too.
A woman raped by her date
won't report it when dating itself is a crime.
She worries about being sentenced guilty,
while her criminal knows he can get away with each woman, each
time.

Criminalizing premarital relationships
creates a system
where men take advantage of women
knowing well those women can't expose
that they were on a date.
The law writes out a guaranteed fate
of no escape
for women to be subject to abuse and rape,
without reporting it,
because if they report
they will be criminalized too.

Talk about a fucking screw!

Criminalizing premarital relationships
doesn't eliminate premarital relationships,
instead it decriminalizes abuse
and rape too-
because it benefits rapists and abusers
and the patriarchy
that they belong to.

1331.

When a member of
a marginalized minority
holds a major position,
all members of
that marginalized minority
are represented.

And when
all members of
marginalized minorities
are represented,
all members of society
are empowered.

                              ***

When you put an abuser
in a position of power;
all abusers will feel safe
to abuse.

When you put a woman
in a position of power;
all women will feel
empowered.

In evil and in good,
the power of representation
must be understood.

1332.

Even if we change
the laws;
if the mindsets
don't change,
nothing changes.

**

Isn't it ironic
how everything liberals believe in
is actually a return to the tradition
of our hunter-gatherer ancestors?
And everything conservatives believe in
is actually the newer progressions
that became norms after?

1333.

You are born a blank slate.

You are not born into patriarchy.
You are not born into a race
or a gender or a sex.
Those things are ascribed
to you by society,
to fit you in a box
with everybody else.

***

Being oppressed
doesn't mean I'll accept
living in oppression

1334.

Everyone talks about the boy who cried wolf
but no one takes about the sheep.

What the fuck is up with y'all sheep?

Why did you just stay there,
on that farm with that liar, and dare
to comfortably go to sleep?
I mean, you knew that boy was a liar
he lied so many times
no one in town
believed him anymore.
Yet you still stuck around
believing he'll keep you secure?!

All you wanted from the boy
was to let you eat and sleep.
But little did y'all know,
that you were the food-
damn you fools
you really are sheep!

N.B. See 2021 storming of the United States Capitol by Trump
supporters.

1335.

Ignorance killed the cat.
Curiosity brought it back.

Read it again.

***

Don't wait for someone to educate you
to spoon feed you.

Be aware and critical
of your traditions and values.

Google the fuck out of that shit
study it
unlearn and relearn
without hesitation.

Stepping out of ignorance
doesn't need an invitation.

***

Whenever I asked my mom about shit
she always told me to Google it
and I thought she was neglecting me.

It took me years to see.

She wanted me to form
my own views
instead of feed her views
to me.

1336.

You learn more about yourself
by what you disagree with
than what you agree with.

That's how you learn more about others too.

***

Yeah sex is cool,
but have you tried
fucking the patriarchy?!

I want casual sex
but not casual sexism.

I want sex every day,
but not everyday sexism.

I want to fuck the patriarchy
but then marry feminism.

I want to give fake phone numbers
but never have fake orgasms.

I want to be proud to be
everything the patriarchy
taught me not to be.

1337.

This is what a feminist looks like:

(Nothing- because our looks have nothing to do with our feminism).

1338.

To be a feminist, you don't have to look a certain way,
there is no guidebook-
fuck what people say.

There are days
where I celebrate my feminine expression like fireworks,
and days where I burn her down because she feels like the cause of
my oppression.

And this hypocrisy
is taught by the patriarchy-
because how can they keep me as a victim
if they don't teach me
how to keep on hating 'me'?

***

We still haven't achieved equality
and we still need feminism for that.
Because if we already achieved equality
feminism won't still be attacked.

1339.

I am not asking man
to make me his equal;
I am already his equal.
I am asking him
simply
to see that.

***

We are equal.

We are equal in the right to exist, to live, and to be free.

And our equality matters
as much as our equity.

1340.

Patriarchy has no headquarters
that we can smash-
it has no
C.E.O.
that we can fire,
or a customer complaint department
that we can go to trash.
Patriarchy is not tangible;
it can be seen, while it remains invisible.
Patriarchy is like polluted air
we breathe it in because it's everywhere-
it seeps into every crack even when
we don't see it there.
Patriarchy penetrates
our languages, our stories,
our traumas, and our territories.
It fucks our laws, and government,
our books, and entertainment.
And even if you strip it off your body
or kick it out of your home,
patriarchy continues to roam-
it stalks you at school,
in the office, and the street.
The only way to smash the patriarchy into defeat-
is by wearing it out
through constant questioning,
wherever you meet.

***

Patriarchy is not some mystical headquarters
located in a far away land
that sprinkles misogyny, racism, homophobia and other evil dust on
earth.

Patriarchy is an infestation
it manifests in every little corner of our lives;
our thoughts, our homes, our schools, our entertainment, our
workplaces, our governments, our societies...

The way to combat it,
is first to be aware of it,
and next dismantle it in your everyday thoughts and actions.

***

The patriarchy systematically puts women
through institutionalized systemic shit,
and we are not only expected to eat it
but to also say it's the yummiest thing we ever ate!
Hands down, no debate!

But shit will always be shit,
no matter how much you sugar-coat it.

1341.

I dream of a world that is inclusive.

In our books, education systems, entertainment, workplaces- I dream of a world that is fair.

I want to see a slice of society included everywhere.

I'm sick of seeing the world in all those spaces be reduced to favour one mould; heterosexual, cis, male, white, abled.

I want gay fairytales in the children books I read to my son.
I want trans teachers in our schools.
I want women in positions of authority.
I want Black peers to fill up my workplace- not just to fill a quota minority.
I want sign language to be an integral part of our education system and incorporated in every TV show.
I want to see the silenced slices of society screaming out of every corner.

And I want them to be heard.

We all make up this world.

***

The future is not female.

Nor is the future male.

Let the present be
about loving one another,
so that the future won't be
for one sex or one gender;
but for healing from a past
that has long passed
yet we still cling,
so its pain will prevail.
The future must be for all of us;
the future will be the present
that we entail.

What are you manifesting for our future?

1342.

He says
"You won't hear me out
because feminism got you believing
every man out there
is out to hate!"

"No" I tell him,
"I won't hear you out
because feminism got me knowing
that my human rights
are not a debate!"

***

Self-reminder:
I am not obliged to hold space
for those who troll and hate.
My human right to exist safely and peacefully
is NOT a debate.

I don't debate
women rights
trans rights
Black rights
gay rights
disability rights.

This isn't a conversation
about whether you agree or disagree

with putting cream or milk in your coffee,
or whether
it's better
to sleep early
or stay up late.

Human rights
are not a debate.

Human rights
aren't only for
the humans
you approve of.
Human rights
include
ALL humans.

Regardless of
sex, race, gender.

Human rights
aren't personal.
Human rights
must be universal.

1343.

Mankind
has dropped the *kind*
to just be a *man*
but you can't be a *man*
without being *kind*.

Mankind.

***

Our blood and bones
have no sex, gender, religion, or race.

The thing that binds us together
is that we are human.

No matter what is our
skin colour
or gender
or sex
or sexual orientation
or religion-
underneath all the narratives
that we have and haven't written,
what binds us together
is that we are human.

Can we focus on that for a minute?

1344.

To win this fight
we need not fight.

***

I want you to reflect.
What human rights matter in our world right now?
What human rights should matter?
How can we close the gap?
Are you listening to your neighbour?
The answers are there, if only we listen.

Let's be mindful of our rights and the rights of others. Because this is
how we heal ourselves. And this is how we heal our world.

I don't want human rights modelled after a cis, White, rich,
heterosexual man. I want human rights that cater to who we each are.

Women rights are human rights.
LGBTQI+ rights are human rights.
Black rights are human rights.
Poor rights are human rights.
Disability rights are human rights.
Sex worker rights are human rights.

Let's make it right!

1345.

The world gazes at me
through the eyes of men,
moulding me
to be desirable to them
shaming me
when I defy them.

I am seen
but not heard.

This how I know
it is a man's world.

                            ***

It is a man's world.

God is a man
and his messengers are men
and the prayer calls at the mosque
are all performed by men.
Jesus is a man,
and Virgin Mary
is only valued for being the mother of a man, without enjoying the
touch of a man.
Santa is a man
and the Elves are men too,
though I am certain it is Ms. Claus that shops for the gifts
and wraps them up too.
So we can see,

women only appear in the story
when they are giving their labour for free.
Peter Pan is a man, and Tarzan is a man
and don't be fooled by Cinderella
stealing the position of star of the show-
for her happy ending is only reached
with a man (as we all know).
Alexander the Great is great
for being a man,
and Cleopatra is great
for being a sex object to man.
And as for me, I lived in a repeated history...
My government,
is a man.
My rapist,
is a man.
My sexist,
boss is a man.
But...But...
My loving husband is a man too.
And if I was totally honest with you,
his gentle love, is enough
to make all women believe
that not all men are controlling.
He always says (and not under duress);
"women must be free too!"...
...But then to my horror I realize
I'm only free
because *a man* allows me to!

1346.

I need men
and not to open jars;
I need men
to fight feminist wars.

***

Men are tired
of me whining about my rights.

You know what I'm tired of?

Men that are tired.

***

We need cooperation
from our oppressor
to end our oppression.

I hate that this is the only way
but history has shown this evidence
for women's progression.

The men must listen
the men must be willing to speak
with us and for us;

this fight isn't women against men
it's patriarchy against all of us.

Like an unborn
trying to exit a womb;
it needs a push from its mother
or a pull from its doctor...
to leave its captivity...
...to finally be free.

This is how we can finally liberate
women and men
and you and me.

1347.

The world only accepts
to hear things from men,
even when the topic isn't about them.

I talk about male-on-female harassment
and I get told I'm just a man-hater.
But when a man talks about the same topic,
he is the heroic messenger
of which only God is greater.

When I say the same things as men-
I get attacked.
It's acceptable only when men
talkback
on behalf of women.

I once fought back a total fucking bellend.

When I narrate the story
I get asked;
"Why did you punch the guy
who groped your ass,
instead of letting your husband do it?"

Screw it.

This world isn't ready
to listen to women,
without men talking over them.
But that doesn't mean I'll stop talking.

My voice may be foreign to the patriarchy-
but I won't remain silent
just because they think I'm provoking.

1348.

What if...
Women actually
invented the patriarchy
and put men at the top of the hierarchy
and made them believe
that they have the power to achieve
anything they want,
just so we can watch them ruin the world
and that's when we come in
to fix all they did wrong
and then claim the prize,
climb the rung
for that is where
we truly belong.
And while men
complain that women
fucked them up,
women will scream "not all women"
as they all sit
at the very top.

N.B. On conspiracy theories

1349.

If we already gave a chance
for men to ruin the world;
why won't we give a chance
for women to run the world?

***

We've been listening to men for so long
without interrupting
without interjecting
without screaming
"WOMAN-HATER".

We've accepted the status quo
walked the path we're told to go
without complaining
without waning
we've internalized this one-man show.

We've been listening to men for so long
this world reeks evidence, of all they did wrong.

We've been listening to men for so long,
it's time we listen to women
without interrupting
without interjecting
without screaming
"MAN-HATER".

It's time we listen to women
this is a world we both live in-
why the fuck are men playing
dictator?

1350.

If you want to heal the world,
heal your relationship with women.

It's the same thing.

***

How humbling it is to realize
that despite the fact that we are all born
from the wombs of different Mothers,
when we die, we will all be laid
into the womb of one Mother...

Mother Earth.

1351.

There is a woman inside me-
trapped inside my body
trapped inside the male gaze
trapped inside misogynistic ways.

There is a woman inside me-
trapped inside
but is actually free;
free from the bondage of sex appeals
free from makeup and high heels
free from existing for men
free from depending on them.

There is a woman inside me-
trapped inside
but is actually free
to be whoever the fuck
she wants to be.
All I have to do
is make her feel safe
to come out
unafraid, undeterred, unapologetic
taking space,
for it's only a man's world
because she's yet to take her place.

***

Women live in
bodies that are

capable of doing so much
yet the patriarchy believes
our bodies exist only to be touched
by men
who want to use us
and reduce us
to sex objects.
My body can do so much more
than what the patriarchy expects.
But they turn all my strengths
into weaknesses,
my beauty
into ugly,
shaming me for bodily
hair and menstruation and a gory childbirth,
convincing me my vagina is a loose hole
when I enjoy lots of sex
erasing my worth,
as a human being
with valid sexual feelings.
It's easier, for sure,
to control someone when you get them to believe they are weak and
insecure.

But what a waste of a life and a body,
if I spend my life
believing
this patriarchy.

***

Don't tell me
I can't do
what men do.

I can go out
past nine,
drink whiskey
and wine,
ask lovers out
to dine,
have an orgasm
every time,
own this body
that is mine.

Don't tell me
I can't do
what men do.
If being a woman
is my crime-
I will buy my freedom
and pay up the fine.

Don't tell me
I can't do
what men do.
Because the only thing that stops me
is that you want me
to believe you.

1352.

I have been waiting.

Waiting for the right time.
Waiting for the love of my life.
Waiting for that big house
publisher to discover my writing.

Waiting.

I have been waiting,
and you know what happens
while you're waiting?

You're just waiting.

Literally.

While you're waiting
you're just waiting.

So if you want things to happen
why the fuck are you *just waiting*?

**

Imagine
if you are the battle and the warrior

you don't need to wait for a saviour.

Imagine
if you are the problem and the solution
the dictator and the revolution,
you don't need to wait for a resolution.

We've been taught to wait for someone to save us
in the movies, and in children stories.

Ask yourself;
If I save myself
instead of waiting for someone else
to save me-
how different today
would my life be?

1353.

This world is built by men
from the oppression
of women.
And then they pretend to save us,
and they want us
to call them 'superheroes'
not 'oppressors'.

Fuck the saviours
when they cause our oppression.

I don't want a world
where men are
attackers and protectors,
and women live
with fairytale hope and faith.

I don't want a world where I'm saved-
I want to be safe.

***

The patriarchy was created by men
and continues because it is upheld by
men with complicity
and women with internalized misogyny.

Are you aware of whether you are participating in
or dismantling this patriarchy?

1354.

Are you surviving oppression
or dismantling oppression?

Surviving means finding ways
to live with it.
Dismantling means finding ways
to destroy it.

Not speaking up to avoid punishment
is a way of surviving.
Justifying
the struggle you feel wearing a hijab
by convincing yourself that it's no big deal
just a cultural garb.
Not going out with your crush because you're not allowed to date
telling yourself that if you're meant to be
it will happen through fate.
Not getting that degree you dream of or that job because that field is
dominated by men
instead you go for something similar but more suited for women.
Those are just a few examples of how
we survive with our oppression.

We sew peace into pieces of pretty embroidery
in order not to disrupt patriarchal fuckery.

In order not to upset your father, your brother, your husband, your
son, your society,
you find ways of surviving
while you're still their property.

But what about you?
Do you believe in that part of the fairytales where dreams can come
true?
Dreams outside of marriage and a baby carriage
dreams outside of being pretty and silent
dreams outside of what patriarchy dreams for you.

You have one life.
Who will you donate it to?

Speak up.
Rip off your hijab.
Pick your own garb.
Go on a date.
Write out your fate.
Get that degree.
Fuck society!

This is how we,
dismantle the patriarchy;
live your life for you
so that the women after you
can live for themselves too.

1355.

I was in a gathering
and the tea was served cold.
I wasn't enjoying it
but no one else complained
so I kept quiet too.

But I really wasn't enjoying drinking
so then I finally decided to say something;
"the tea is cold I'm not enjoying it"
I said,
"I'd like for it to be
replaced with hot tea
instead".

"Me too!" said my mother.
"Me too!" said my sister.
"Me too, me too", all the other women said.

And then as we all got the tea replaced
I realized
all you ever need to do
is speak out...
that's how you encourage others to do the same
and that's how you make change.

Speak out if you don't like your tea.
Speak out for you and for me.

We can save the world.

We can make a change one by one,

and that's the only way
it can be done.

1356.

If I can pay my bills
with your opinions,
I'll take them!

But I know that I can't.

And I don't have any time
for any fucks
to give.
What I have is
a certain unknown
number of years
to live.

***

What is the price I paid
to be free?

Let's see,
I have collected those invoices
mountains of receipts
to show my future daughter
how much it cost
to be me.

There's family
I lost

and there's friends too.
There's trolls
I've gained
and lots of haters too.

I pay (from my already unequal pay)
every day
for the glares I get
when I go out
wearing whatever I want,
either because I'm showing too much skin
or because I too proudly flaunt
a not-so-ideal curvy body.
I can't count the debt I'm in
all the price tags
society wraps
around my ribs,
for the countless times
I've loved my body
as it is.
I don't want cosmetic surgery
or makeup or corsets
or high heels.
Accepting yourself as you are
at the size and height that you are
almost feels,
like oppression
to your oppressor-
they can't believe you don't seek validation
from their scale or their mirror
to be thinner, to be thicker, to be better,
oh the horror!
They can't believe

you won't pay to achieve
the perfect hair, the perfect body,
so they make you pay in other ways
by treating you like a nobody.
You don't get their praise
you don't fit the male gaze
you don't fit in
but my darling, lift up your double chin.

The only love you need, is the one you don't have to pay for-
the only love you need, is found within.

Let's burn
those receipts that
keep us in debt to a history
where no one is invested
in a woman's misery,
everyone just pays to listen
to the men's side of the story.

I know I will be shamed,
but I will not be sorry.

I'll continue to pay the price
of being me,
until my future daughter's mortgage
is paid off
and she will be free, for free.

1357.

For this new year
I don't want to be
a new me.

I have no resolution.
I have no plan.
I have no desire,
to renovate who I am.

No new diet or gym membership.
No one hundred fuckboy dates
just to settle for one relationship.
Fuck relationships that act like gym memberships;
they sign up once, fuck you twice,
then disappear without even saying
they're not committed.

Fuck societal checklists,
where my happiness is omitted.

For this new year
I don't want to be
a new me.
Instead, I want to meet the me
that I've neglected.

I want to welcome her home
for the very first time.
And allow her to take back
all her lost time.
I want to take her out

for a walk, for a date,
for a glass of wine.
I want to admire the way
her curves, and stretch marks,
and cellulite
rhyme.

For this new year
I don't want to be
a new me.

I don't want to find a new way.

For this new year
I want to come home.
And this time,
I actually want to stay.

***

They tell you self-love is selfish
so we all walk around with open wounds
that ooze pain onto others
waiting to be given the love
that we didn't get from our mothers and fathers.

But what if we loved ourselves
instead of expecting everyone else
to love us while we're unlovable?
What if we put bandages on our blood
instead of expecting others to drink it while it's destructible?

What if self-love isn't selfish
and you take that to be true-
what if what's selfish is demanding
that others love
the worst version of you?

What if we love our own selves
a little louder, a little stronger
and make self-love the norm.

Our world needs healing
but how can we heal it
if we can't even heal on our own?

1358.

What if
I am the one
I've been waiting for?

Not that great career.
Not that great love.
Not that great man.
Not that great wedding or baby or family tree...

What if
all I ever need
is to recognize the greatness that is me?

***

We search
for "the One"
to love us
the way we want to
love ourselves,
instead of just...
loving ourselves.

I hope you could see
that self-love
is the greatest love story
you will ever live;
because you'll finally be taking
what you always give.

I hope you could see
that you,
are the best thing
to happen
to you.

1359.

"What's your favourite colour?"
they ask.

Why can't they all be my favourite colours?
I think.

What's your favourite food? Music? Friend? Lover? Sex position?

Why can't it be all of it?
Why can't we be multi-dimensional
instead of being forced to pick
one dimension?

***

Do
raise your voice.
Do not
lower your values.

There is enough room
for all the women
you want to be.

1360.

I see the world
through the same window sill.

Still.

The same sky.

Nothing changed.

Except I.

When did I stop seeing the world
through the eyes of a child?
I saw the moon stalking me.
I saw every tree
dance with the wind.
I saw lovers
out of birds and their cries.
I saw silence
with my own eyes.

When did I stop believing in magic?
When did I start believing lies?

I don't remember
mourning the child I was.

But I do remember
the hurried goodbyes.

***

I've become
the role model
I needed
when I was younger.

Perhaps we all just need to grow
into the superheroes that we know
we needed
when we were
younger.

Perhaps that's how
we make the world better.

1361.

"When did you become a feminist?"
they ask.

"I was born a feminist" I reply.

No baby girl would ever cry
because she hates her body.
No baby girl is born
doubting her own
ability.
No baby girl is born
seeing herself as inferior.
It is a patriarchal society
that taught me
boys and men are superior.

I saw no other
stronger person than my mother.
She carries oceans
in her tear drops.
When I doubt myself,
she'd tell me to "woman up!".
And when she was stopped
from whatever she wanted to do
and told that women aren't allowed
to do what men can always do,
she'd tell them
she's worth a thousand men,
using their yardstick to measure her worth
because that's the only language
they understand.

She taught me that the world thinks men are strong because they bark
commands,
but it is the women that lift the weight of the world
with their bare hands.

Don't ask me when did I become a feminist
because every girl and woman is
born loving herself.

Instead ask me
when did I realize that the patriarchy
was teaching me
to doubt myself?

1362.

She wrote me
telling me
she wanted one of my books so bad,
but she feared that if her father sees it
he'll be mad
at her
for reading about female pleasure
revolutions and feminism,
liberating herself
from the jail of his oppression.
She said she dreams of the day that she's old enough
to pack up all her stuff
and move out
she'll then unpack all my books
without a doubt.

I wrote back to her
telling her;
dreams do come true,
I was you, too,
not allowed to read, so I started writing.
I understand the sadness you're living
but the fact that you can see a happy ending,
means you're already fighting.

1363.

I think I figured out
why art
nourishes the soul.

Not just for me, for us all.

I enjoy
writing poetry
watching movies
getting lost in an art gallery,
because it forces me
to sit in the moment
in the now
in the today.

For in every other aspect of my life
I'm either in the tomorrow
or the yesterday.

***

Science
keeps us alive
but art,
is what we live for.

And love,

is what we die for.

***

If we were all doctors
and lawyers
and teachers...
who will be
the artists
the activists
and the love
preachers?

Each one of us has value.

Each one of us has work to do
that can impact
this world.

Each one of us has a voice,
how are you making
yours heard?

***

And I hope you realize,
your impact isn't about your size.

A single strand of hair on your tongue
can make you choke.

A tiny prick from a pin
can pierce blood from your skin.

A drop of soap can burn your eyes.

Impact isn't about size.

No matter how small the step you take
I hope you realize;
your impact isn't about your size.

1364.

I hope there will come a time
in my lifetime
where I won't need to spend my time
fighting for the rights of women all the time.

I hope there will come a time
in my lifetime
where I can spend my time
with just pleasure and bliss;
not worrying about being a warrior
or a princess.

***

I write
for a future
hoping they won't need
to read
what I write.

This is what it's like living
with the hope
for which you fight.

1365.

I am the daughter
of a revolution.

Of diamond lips
sealed with blood,
of lotus beauty
growing out of mud.

I am the daughter
of women
that have moved on
and moved this world
with the stories they lived
yet no one heard.

I write what we're afraid to feel.

I write to create bandages
for all of us to heal.

I am the daughter
of a revolution,
and I have already
signed a deal
with the future
of my daughter
so that her daughter
can live
without being afraid
to feel.

***

Sometimes you need to say
the same things
differently.

For the world needs to see
the same things
differently.

1366.

I want to create a world
where fairytales don't have to end
with a prince kissing a princess,
but with whatever feels like
your happily ever after.

That is the world I'm after.

***

You think happiness will come
after that graduate degree,
but then the degree comes
and happiness doesn't.

You think happiness will come
after that big promotion,
but then the promotion comes
and happiness doesn't.

You think happiness will come
after that great love story,
but then the love comes
and happiness doesn't.

You think happiness will come
after that happy ending marriage,
but then the marriage comes
and happiness doesn't.

You think happiness will come
after you orgasm,
but you don't realize that happiness *comes*
while you orgasm.

1367.

We all come from stories.

We are all born into stories.

Upon storeys.
Upon storeys.

We are all the main character
in our own book,
and perhaps just a chapter
in someone else's book.

What's your hook?

What's your climax?

How's your life pending?

Remember that
we each have
the same beginning
and the same ending.

***

We don't remember how
we took our first breath.
And we don't know how
we'll take our last breath.

Perhaps that is why
we take each breath
for granted.

1368.

Words can kill you
or they can set you free.

Which words are you speaking?
Which words are you hearing?

What will it be?

**

You are the author
of your life story.

When they try to grab that pen
from your hand
when they edit your chapters
in ways you don't understand-
snatch that goddamn
pen back!

You are not meant to be
the side track,
of your own plot.

You are the author, the hero, the creator-
whether they like it or not!

1369.

We're all just here on transit,
might as well make the best of it.

***

I tattoo
this black ink
onto this cream paper
to leave my words here
forever.

***

The only regret I have in life
is that I have not sinned more often
I have not broken rules more often
I have more often accepted my oppression
I have tiptoed around my real life desires
I have made my life hell
for the promise of a ticket to an imaginary heaven...

1370.

It should not be a privilege for women to have rights.
Rights are not a privilege.
Rights are rights.

***

Understand that
your rights as a woman
are not something you have to wait
for someone to give to you-
they are born with you
they are yours
like your body
like your voice.

No one can take your power;
giving it away
is your choice.

1371.

Patriarchy discourages women
from having ownership
of their own bodies;
we are told how to dress
we are taught to say yes
we are trained to impress
we are made lovable
only when we accept
to make ourselves available
for sex.

Our bodies are used to service
the patriarchy;
to pleasure men
and to carry their seed for them.

That is why we are shamed
when we claim ownership
of our own bodies;
when we decide how to dress
when we say "no" instead of "yes"
when we don't care to impress
when we don't seek to be lovable
and instead love
the way we love to have sex.

When we don't use our bodies to service
the patriarchy;
when we destroy the gender hierarchy
when we find pleasure with other women
or when we get an abortion

or when we decide not to let men
make us wives
when we make our own rules
for our lives,
they shame us because they realize
that shame is the only grip
they have left to hold onto.
So to break free from them
all that we must do
is unlearn the hurt we feel from shame.
This is how we heal our pain
and end their game.

***

The purpose
of this
body that I'm wearing
is to function, to serve me,
but instead-
the patriarchy has it reduced
to a sex object, to be used,
by fuckboys in bed.

1372.

Anatomical autonomy
is necessary
for women to be free;
to make decisions
about our body
to embrace modesty
or to be revealed
to have sex or not
to have an abortion
when we want
to not have
our genitals cut
in the name of traditions
to not be abused or raped
or blamed
to not need permission
or to be shamed
for being fat or thin
to paint or not to paint
our hair and skin.

To be or not to be?
No question about
our anatomical autonomy.

1373.

It's okay to gain weight
not because you're
going through
a Coronavirus pandemic,
but because you're human.

It's okay to feel stressed
not because you're
going through
a Coronavirus pandemic,
but because you're human.

It's okay to just want to rest
not because you're
going through
a Coronavirus pandemic,
but because you're human.

It's okay to be human
not because you're
going through
a Coronavirus pandemic,
but because you're human.

***

It's okay.

It's okay to wear a short dress
without shaving your legs,
to not marry that guy
your parents think is the best.

It's okay.

It's okay to have sex
with whoever you want,
or to get an abortion
or to proudly flaunt
that you're gay or asexual
or bi.
It's okay to eat an entire
portion of apple pie.

In the end, we're all going
to die.

It's okay to live life
however you dream,
and it's okay if you seem
strange to someone else.

What matters the most is
do you feel *okay* with yourself?

It's okay.

It's okay.

Farida D.

It's okay.

***

The freedom that comes
with not giving a shit
is how we dismantle
the power of patriarchy-
and that's actually
the only way to do it!

1374.

I'm in a prison,
but the doors are unlocked
but when I try to get out
the guards push me back in.

They tell me I'm free
they unlock the doors for me;
but I am still in prison.

A prison in which no one can feel
what I see.

This is what it feels like when they tell me "you have your rights!"
while they still oppress me
with all their might.

***

Internalized oppression
is when you're caged in a prison
but you're given
the key.
Yet you don't leave
because you don't believe
you have the right
to be free.

***

Telling a victim to
"stop playing victim"
is by far
the worst kind
of victim blaming.

They victimize me
then tell me
to stop *playing* victim.

And as I weep
for my life
for my sisters
for fate of our DNA,
all I can say:

I wish it was all
a play.

N.B. I won't stop till the curtains' up.

1375.

"You attract this to yourself"
he says.

When I share simple experiences
of being a human,
that aren't safe for women to do.
When even going out for a walk at night, or crossing the road isn't
safe-
it is victim blaming to assume I'm bringing this to myself.
Men need to do their part- no excuses, no fuss.
This world is for all of us.

                            ***

Men are safe
walking around
topless
in a world full of heterosexual women
not because women have no sexual desire;
but because women
are conditioned
to restrain
their sexual desire.

1376.

Who says women aren't free?

We're free.

We're free to be angry
but we must be
polite
while we're angry.

We're free to have voices
but we must whisper
while using them.

We're free to wear whatever we want
but we must accept
our bodies to be violated by any man
whenever he wants.

Who says women aren't free?

We're free.

But that freedom
comes with expenses.

We're free
but only in the way
men approve of us to be,
otherwise
we must suffer the consequences.

***

You can make your own choices
you are free,
so long as
your choices agree
with me.

N.B. Patriarchal democracy.

1377.

Perhaps we never heal from trauma.
Perhaps we just learn a new normal.
Perhaps we just learn how to continue navigating in life while trying
so hard to pretend that the trauma never happened.
Perhaps we fake it till we make it.
Perhaps we never make it.
Perhaps faking it is how we make it.
Perhaps there isn't a bridge to cross from victimhood to the land of
survivor.
Perhaps we burn the bridge.
Perhaps we are the bridge.
Perhaps we take it day by day.
Perhaps we take it step by step.
Yes that's what it is.
Step by step.
Perhaps.

1378.

Let what you've
passed through,
pass through.

It's called the 'past' for a reason.

You'll feel hot and heavy
if you carry
your winter clothes
into the summer season.

***

When we refuse to heal
our toxic fumes
are exhaled
into the air around us,
then inhaled
by everyone around us.

When we refuse to heal
we suffocate
we hurt ourselves
and everyone around us.

N.B. For reference, look at what Trump has done.

1379.

Mental hell.
Mental hel.
Mental help.
Mental heal.
Mental health.

1380.

Unlearn and heal,
Little One.

Unlearn and heal,
this life is meant
for fun.

Your bones carry the memory
of the pain of your ancestry,
all your anxiety
is a sign from your mind and body
wanting to break free
from a million centuries
of expectations and oppressions.

The way to make your life hell
is by waiting to go to heaven.

There's no waiting-
if there's a heaven
it is only here and now.

You want to get there?
Here's how:

You don't have to be
what they moulded your mother as.

Unlearn and heal,
to be yourself at last-
history repeats itself,

only if you don't learn from the past.

1381.

My body is my God.
My bath tub is my temple.
Relaxing is my prayer.
The bath is my sacred sanctuary.
It is where I rinse the sins
of patriarchy
off my skin,
and touch my holy soul
with holy water.

My body is my God
and I am her daughter.

***

My body belongs to me.

I refuse to give up ownership of my body.

Not to my father
Not to my husband.
Not to my government.
Not to my God.

My body is not a mortgage
and I will not live in debt
waiting to be free.

***

Reclaiming our bodies (in whatever way- from our weight to our wombs, to what we wear or how we groom, or who and how we fuck) is punished (in so many ways- from shaming to blaming, to rules and regulations, to violence and death) because the patriarchy has colonized women's bodies. From father, to husband, to government, to God; women's bodies are always controlled by, and thus, belong to someone other than the actual owner. Our bodies are colonized to the extent that reclaiming our bodies is punished as if we are stealing something that isn't innately ours.

How are you decolonizing your body?

1382.

And let it be known
that wombs are not machines
that you put sperm into
to multiply your ego
to make more men
to make more of you,
because that's the only gender
you truly value.

1383.

Dear Belle,
you didn't have to
save the Beast.

I wish you hadn't
saved the Beast.
I wish you hadn't
taught me that
it's my job
to make a prince
out of a fuckboy.

I wonder what
happened to the libraries
that gave you true joy.

Did you give up reading
for a man who never read
the song of your soul
or the dreams in your bed?
I wish the story ended
by you showing me
what you can do
when you follow your heart.
Instead of sacrificing your all
to make others whole
out of each part,
of you.

Self-love isn't selfish,
I wish

you knew this.
And I wish
you taught me this
too.
Because I've spent so many years
picking my dreams out of the dreams
that society wants for me
to come true.

Dear Belle,
you didn't have to
save the Beast.

I wish you just saw that,
at the very least.

1384.

Why do badass women
settle for mediocre men?

I'll tell you why.
Because badassery
in our society
isn't seen as a
fucking fiercely fine quality
for a woman.
She is either Mrs. or Miss.
so she boards the mediocre train
because she doesn't want to *Miss* it.

And the sad part is
that she would actually know,
that train she settled in
isn't going
anywhere she wants to go.

But she doesn't get off
because she's taught that
settling in the company of the train
is better than standing alone
on that platform again.

Get up.
Get off.
The next stop
is calling your name.

You are not alone, and never will be.

Because you packed with you
all your badassery.

1385.

He is the kind of man
that you have to constantly fight to keep.

There is no victory.

If you stop fighting you face defeat.

Do you want a relationship where you never stop fighting?

1386.

His bodily hair would shed
on our bed
during sex.

Perhaps that's what it takes
to transform a man
from *Beast*
to a *Beauty*.

***

I felt closest to him
when we have sex
because it was only during sex
that we had any intimacy.

Our relationship was starving
for a climax
built up
from a foreplay
of misery.

***

But wait.

Is the sex actually great,
or is it bait?

The dentist
that gives the kids
lollipops
keeps them
coming back.

And they come back
not because they want to,
but because they *need* to.

1387.

He wants me to gag
on his dick
and tell him how big it is,
and I want him to gag
on my mind
and tell me how big it is.

***

I don't care about
how long you can last in bed.

Tell me
how long will you last in my life?

1388.

Come on in,
if you want.

Or go,
if you want.

But don't crack my door open halfway
and stand there in my doorway.

I'm in for the long haul
not for the hallway.

1389.

To revenge him,
I slept with another man.

Even though I didn't want to,
I just wanted to show him that I can
too.

The only problem with this,
is
that to revenge *him* by giving *my body* away
means that I inherently believe
my body is his.

1390.

I don't understand the idea
of the "revenge body".

If to revenge my man
I have to be "smaller" than
I used to be-
is the revenge on him?
Or it is it on me?

1391.

There's three of us
in this bed.

You, me,
and the lies you said.

1392.

A fuckboy
that keeps saying:
But
I'm a man!
I'm a man!
I'm a man!

Sounds like
a toddler
that keeps saying:
But
I'm a grown-up!
I'm a grown-up!
I'm a grown-up!

If he has to say it
because he's aware
that you can't see it-
then clearly,
he's not it.

1393.

It is not my job
to make you "feel like a man".
I will not shrink
for you to rise.

At the end of each day
the sun sets in her sky
for the moon to shine his armour
showing off his power
feeling mighty
over the tiny twinkly
stars in the skies.

But it only takes for the sun to rise
again
for the moon to realize,
that his light comes from the sun
and his power is just a disguise.

1394.

There were so many red flags.

But red
was my favourite colour.

***

In a red dress.

Displaying my meat
to make ends meet.

Red is the colour
of war and defeat.

A red c-section scar
below
my hips.
A red flowing stream
between
my lips.

My red disgusts
unless,
it is a red lipstick
or a mini-dress.

Now red is sexy
oh yes.

When it's displayed on my meat
to make ends meet.

And to what they see
I retreat.

Red is the colour
of seduction and treat.

Red flags everywhere
but I still go for another.

Because he told me that red
is his favourite colour.

1395.

You say
you want me,
but
you stay
when it's easy
and you run
when it gets tough-
Boy, my heart is not on the Stock Exchange
bought when the price is low
sold when the price goes up.

1396.

Men want women to be their mothers;
to cook and clean for them
and pacify them,
but our vaginas are the pacifiers
where their penises would tuck.

But we should be more like their fathers;
don't expect us to be doing any housework
and we decide when it's time to fuck!

***

In a toxic relationship
a man is looking for a woman
who behaves like his mother;
forgiving him
for all his unforgiveable mistakes.
While a woman is looking for a man
who behaves like her father;
she accepts his abuse
no matter what the stakes.

1397.

I want a man.

I don't want a boy
who just left the womb
wanting me to mother
his wounds
to nurse
his broken bone
with my full chest,
to offer him the best
day-care service
with
no fees
no rules,
and at night
be his comfort blanket
while he drools.

I'm done shrinking
for boys to walk tall on my back.

I want my body and my life back.

I know that I deserve it, I know that I can;
instead of nurse boys,
I want to walk tall
beside a man.

***

I need the love of a man
who tastes like fine wine
and feels like the glory
of reaching the peak of a mountain top.

Not a man who reeks of beer
expecting me to hold his weight
as I barely bear
how heavy he is
because he just wants to be on top.

1398.

Girls are taught they are incomplete
without a prince.
But boys are taught
the opposite of this.

So boys grow up to become entitled men
confident that a woman
will always be
waiting for them,
forgiving them
no matter how many times they fuck up.

This fucking narrative has to stop.

A girl must be taught that she doesn't need a prince
for her life to be in alignment-
and a boy must learn that to be with a princess
his life must first be in alignment.

1399.

Enough telling women to wait for men,
as if the most important thing a woman can be is a wife.
Enough telling women to cater to men,
as if that's the most important thing a woman can do with her life.

I will not
raise my daughter
to wait for a prince.
Why doesn't the prince
ever wait for when the princess is ready?!

Women have dragons to fight too
and ceilings to shatter
and dreams, beyond marriage, that matter-
we're not born to bake cake and fold laundry.

Why hasn't it occurred to the world
that a woman's life is not a transit
for men who aren't in a hurry?

1400.

Women are waiting.

Not for men to love us.
Not for men to save us.
Not for men to call us pretty.
Not for men's pity
for women under the patriarchy.

Women are waiting.

Not for men to be Adam
only to blame it all on Eve.
Not for men to be saviour
only to gaslight and deceive.

Women are waiting.

For when we are speaking
women are waiting,
for men to believe.

To the one holding this book;
To make the world better...
hold your sister.

And believe her.